D0952934

"You're about to gain some fresh insight into some of the mysteries of masculinity. *For Women Only* is a book that I believe will provide understanding and bring harmony to a lot of marriages."

—BOB LEPINE
Cohost of *FamilyLife Today*

"Ready for an eye-opener? Shaunti Feldhahn has uncovered a mountain of meaningful information for any woman wanting to understand men at a profound level."

—DRS. LES AND LESLIE PARROTT
Seattle Pacific University
Authors of *Love Talk*

"What an important book!"

—BETH MOORE
Author and speaker

"If you want to know what makes your man tick, *For Women Only* is the book for you. Feldhahn provides solid research findings to support seven revelations about the inner lives of men that have the potential to revolutionize your marriage!"

—BOB RECCORD
President of North American Mission Board

"*For Women Only* is the simplest, yet most profound marriage book I've ever read. Inside this little book is the power to change you and your relationship."

—LISA WHELCHEL
Author of the bestselling *Creative Correction* and
The Facts of Life and Other Lessons My Father Taught Me

for women only

what you need to know
about the inner lives of men

by Shaunti Feldhahn

Multnomah® Publishers
Sisters, Oregon

FOR WOMEN ONLY
published by Multnomah Publishers, Inc.
Published in association with the literary agency of
Calvin Edwards, 1220 Austin Glen Drive, Atlanta, GA 30338
© 2004 by Veritas Enterprises, Inc.

International Standard Book Number: 1-59052-317-2

Cover design by David Carlson Design
Cover art by Veer Incorporated
Author photo by Melissa Fortenbery at One Click Away, Buford, Georgia.
Interior design and typeset by Katherine Lloyd, The DESK, Bend, Oregon

Unless otherwise indicated, Scripture quotations are from:
Holy Bible, New Living Translation
© 1996. Used by permission of Tyndale House Publishers, Inc.
All rights reserved.

Multnomah is a trademark of Multnomah Publishers, Inc.,
and is registered in the U.S. Patent and Trademark Office.
The colophon is a trademark of Multnomah Publishers, Inc.

Printed in the United States of America

For information:
MULTNOMAH PUBLISHERS, INC.
POST OFFICE BOX 1720
SISTERS, OREGON 97759

06 07 08 09 10—19 18 17 16 15 14

For Jeff,
my beloved, my friend.

SONG OF SOLOMON 5:16

Contents

Chapter 1

LIGHTBULB ON!

How I Woke Up to What I Didn't Know About Men

The other half of the people on the planet already know what you're going to read in this book.

As newlyweds, my husband and I lived in Manhattan, and like all New Yorkers we walked everywhere. But I quickly noticed something strange. Quite often we'd be strolling hand in hand and Jeff would abruptly jerk his head up and away. We'd be watching in-line skaters in Central Park or waiting to cross the street in a crowd, and he would suddenly stare at the sky. I started to wonder, *Is something going on at the tops of these buildings?*

Turns out, something *was* going on, but it wasn't up in the buildings.

9

Have you ever been totally confused by something the man in your life has said or done? Have you ever wondered, looking at his rapidly departing back, *Why did that make him so angry?* Have you ever been perplexed by your husband's defensiveness when you ask him to stop working so much? Yeah? Me too.

But now, after conducting spoken and written interviews with more than one thousand men, I can tell you that the answers to those and dozens of other common perplexities are all related to what is going on in your man's inner life. Most are things he wishes you knew but doesn't know how to tell you. In some cases, they're things he has no idea you don't know. This book will share those interviews and those answers. But be careful, ladies. You might be slapping your forehead a lot!

> I can tell you that the answers to dozens of other common perplexities are related to what is going on in your man's inner life.

HOW IT ALL STARTED...

Let me tell you how I got here. It all started with the research for my second novel, *The Lights of Tenth Street*. One of the main characters was a man, a devoted, godly husband

and father. Because I wanted this character's thought life to closely resemble what real men deal with, I interviewed my husband, Jeff, and many other male friends to try to get inside their heads. It took me a while to figure out how to handle what I found.

You see, in the novel my character had a secret struggle: He loved his wife and kids and was a devoted follower of Christ, but he liked looking at women and had a constant battle with his thought life. A constant day-by-day, even minute-by-minute battle with the temptations that beckoned from every corner of our culture, from the secret traps of the Internet to the overt appeal of the miniskirt walking down the street.

In short—and this is what was such a surprise to me—instead of being unusual, my character was like almost every man on the planet. Including the devoted Christian husbands I was interviewing.

That revelation led to others, on a half-dozen other subjects, and following those trails led to the hundreds of personal and written interviews with men—including a professional survey—that form the core of this book. I interviewed close friends over dinner and strangers in the grocery store, married fathers at church and the single student sitting next to me on the airplane. I talked to CEOs, attorneys, pastors, technology geeks, business managers, the security guard at Costco, and the guys behind the counter at Starbucks. I even interviewed a professional opera singer and a former NFL offensive tackle with a Super Bowl ring. No one was safe.

Lightbulb on!

It turned out that these men shared some surprisingly common inner wiring. At their secret inner core, many had similar fears and concerns, feelings and needs.

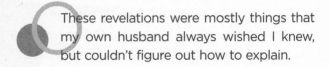

These revelations were mostly things that my own husband always wished I knew, but couldn't figure out how to explain.

I discovered that there were many things I thought I understood about men—but really didn't. In several areas, my understanding was purely surface-level. Once I got below the surface and into specifics, everything changed. I felt like a cartoon character who suddenly had a lightbulb over my head.

Even better, it turned out that those revelations were mostly about things that my own husband always wished I knew but couldn't figure out how to explain. And that was a common refrain from most of the men I talked to. Although I still make many mistakes in my relationship with my husband—and will continue to!—finally grasping these things has hopefully helped me to better appreciate and support him in the way that *he* needs.

I want that lightbulb to go on for you as well.

> We all know, for example, that "men are visual," but, well...what exactly does that *mean*?

Why was this surprising?

In a way, I was surprised to be so...surprised. We women think we know many things about a man's inner life. We all know, for example, that "men are visual," but, well...what exactly does that *mean*?

It turns out that what that means *in practice* is the key thing—the specific insight that will help you be a better wife, girlfriend, or mother. Using the "visual" example, the difference is vast between having the vague notion that men are visual and knowing that the sexy commercial he just watched has become a mental time bomb that will rise up and assault him the next day. The difference is vast between helplessly wondering what is going on in his head and having the insight of hundreds of men to help you understand not only what is going on, but also how to support him.

Actually, there was a kind of double surprise in this research. When I interviewed men and drew some conclusions, they would often say, "But women already know that...surely they know *that*." All too frequently, I found myself replying, "Well, *I* didn't know that." I began to realize that there's so much about men that we don't understand—and that men don't even know we don't know. And that sort of misunderstanding is the stuff that gives birth to a lot of conflict.

SEVEN REVELATIONS

So here are the revelations this book is going to cover—seven translations from "surface level" to "in practice" that you, like me, may not have realized before.

As with all of us, the inner life of a man is a package, with these elements melded and wrapped up inside. Whether you are relating to a husband, boyfriend, or son, it is impossible to understand one part of his inner life in isolation. Every area affects every other area, and I'm only covering those few areas that I thought were the most important or helpful.

The survey

Thankfully, these revelations are also backed up by evidence—a groundbreaking professional survey of hundreds of men.

Our Surface Understanding	What That Means in Practice
"Men need respect"	➡ Men would rather feel unloved than inadequate and disrespected.
"Men are insecure"	➡ Despite their "in control" exterior, men often feel like impostors and are insecure that their inadequacies will be discovered.
"Men are providers"	➡ Even if you personally made enough income to support the family's lifestyle, it would make no difference to the mental burden he feels to provide.
"Men want more sex"	➡ Your sexual desire for your husband profoundly affects his sense of well-being and confidence in all areas of his life.
"Men are visual"	➡ Even happily married men struggle with being pulled toward live and recollected images of other women.
"Men are unromantic clods"	➡ Actually, most men enjoy romance (sometimes in different ways) and want to be romantic—but hesitate because they doubt they can succeed.
"Men care about appearance"	➡ You don't need to be a size 3, but your man does need to see you making the effort to take care of yourself—and he will take on significant cost or inconvenience in order to support you.

Since I found no survey data like this on the market, two sets of experts, Chuck Cowan at Analytic Focus, the former chief of survey design at the U.S. Census Bureau, and Cindy Ford and the survey team at Decision Analyst, came together to help me conduct this survey. The survey was blind, done at random, and meticulously planned and executed. Four hundred anonymous men across the country, ranging in age from twenty-one to seventy-five, answered two dozen questions about their lives and about how they think, what they feel, and what they need. The survey stressed that we weren't dealing with outward behavior as much as with the inner thoughts and emotions that led to their behavior.

Later, because the survey itself inevitably led to additional revelations, I conducted a more informal follow-up survey of another four hundred anonymous men—this time, specifically churchgoers—to ask a few additional questions (and some of the same ones). And later yet, I validated several of those additional insights with a second Decision Analyst survey. Amazingly, across all these surveys there were very few differences.

After all the surveying, the results of my personal interviews were confirmed. Not only had I heard the same things over and over—quotes that I will include in the following pages—but those anecdotal results were now backed up by statistically valid evidence. I *hadn't* just happened to interview the hundred weirdest men on the planet! (Since I am an analyst and not a psychologist, and since my grad-school statistics professor might politely question the statistical skills of someone who needed a whole semester to learn regression analysis, I was quite relieved that professional statisticians confirmed my findings!)

Results were backed up by statistically valid evidence. I hadn't just happened to interview the hundred weirdest men on the planet!

In the end, the men I spoke with and surveyed appear to have been extremely transparent and honest about some very personal subjects. So, men—whoever you are—I thank you.

BEFORE WE START: GROUND RULES

You're probably rarin' to turn the page, but before you get to look inside the inner lives of men, here are some ground rules:

- First, if you are looking for male-bashing or proof that your husband is indeed a cad, you won't find it here. I honor the men who shared their hearts with me, and I hope that by sharing their insight, more women might come to understand and appreciate the wonderful differences between us.

If you are looking for male-bashing or proof that your husband is indeed a cad, you won't find it here.

- Second, this is not an equal treatment of male-female differences, nor do I deal at all with how your man can or should relate to *you*. Yes, we women obviously also have needs, and many of the truths discussed in these pages apply to us too. But since the theme is the inner lives of *men* and my space is limited, I'm focusing entirely on how we relate to men, not the other way around. (That is also why the survey did not poll gay men.)

- Third, recognize that there are always exceptions to every rule. When I say that "most men" appear to think a certain way, realize that "most" means exactly that—most, not all. I'm making generalizations out of necessity, and inevitably there will be exceptions. One reason I did the professional survey was to determine what was an exception and what was normal.

- Fourth, I'm addressing what is normal *inside* men, not necessarily what is right in their outward behavior. And since these pages are not the place for a lengthy exploration of any one issue, you can always go to www.4-womenonly.com to explore more resources, including the entire survey.

- Fifth, I need to warn you that some of the enclosed insight may be distressing because it affects our view of the men in our lives and our view of ourselves. It was tempting to exclude certain things, but I realized that I was hearing things men often weren't willing or able to say directly to their spouses or girlfriends. So it was critical to include these comments. But please realize that in most cases, these comments have little to do with *us*— they are just the way men are wired. And we should celebrate that fact. After all, it is *because he is wired as a man* that you love him.

> The more we understand the men in our lives, the better we can support and love them in the way they need to be loved.

- Finally, and most important, I hope that this book is not just about learning fascinating new secrets. The more we understand the men in our lives, the better we can support and love them in the way they need to be loved. In other words, this revelation is supposed to change and improve *us*.

So read on, ladies, and join me as we look into the inner lives of men.

Chapter 2

YOUR LOVE IS *NOT* ENOUGH

Why Your Respect Means More to Him than Even Your Affection

Men would rather feel alone and unloved than inadequate and disrespected.

When I was a year or two out of college, I went on a retreat that profoundly impacted my understanding of men. The theme of the retreat was "Relationships," which as you can imagine was of great interest to a group of single young adults.

For the very first session, the retreat speaker divided the room in half and placed the men on one side, women on the other.

"I'm going to ask you to choose between two bad things," he said. "If you had to choose, would you rather feel alone and unloved in the world OR would you rather feel inadequate and disrespected by everyone?"

I remember thinking, *What kind of choice is that? Who would ever choose to feel unloved?*

The speaker then turned to the men's side of the room. "Okay, men. Who here would rather feel alone and unloved?"

A sea of hands went up, and a giant gasp rippled across the women's side of the room.

He asked which men would rather feel disrespected, and we women watched in bemusement as only a few men lifted their hands.

Then it was our turn to answer and the men's turn to be shocked when most of the women indicated that they'd rather feel inadequate and disrespected than unloved.

The speaker asked the men, "Who would rather feel unloved?" A sea of hands went up.

WHAT IT MEANS

While it may be totally foreign to most of us, the male need for respect and affirmation—especially from his woman—is so hardwired and so critical that most men would rather feel unloved than disrespected or inadequate. The survey indicated that *three out of four men* would make that choice. Look at the survey results:

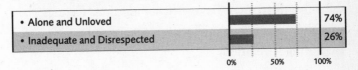

Think about what these two negative experiences would be like: to feel alone and unloved in the world OR to feel inadequate and disrespected by everyone. If you were forced to choose one, which would you prefer? Would you rather feel...? [Choose One Answer]

• Alone and Unloved	74%
• Inadequate and Disrespected	26%

0%   50%   100%

When I originally tested the survey questions, I was perplexed that many men had a hard time answering the "unloved versus disrespected" question—because they appeared to equate the two. Chuck Cowan, the survey-design expert, warned me that might happen. *Why?* I wondered. *Those are two totally different things!* Then one of my readers tested my survey questions on ten men who didn't know me. When I got the surveys back, only one note was attached: "A lot of the guys fussed over Question 3 [the question above]. They did not feel the choices were different."

Finally, the lightbulb came on: *If a man feels disrespected, he is going to feel unloved.* And what that translates to is this: <u>If you want to love your man in the way *he* needs to be loved, then you need to ensure that he feels your respect most of all.</u>

The funny thing is—most of us *do* respect the man in

our lives and often don't realize when our words or actions convey exactly the opposite! We may be totally perplexed when our man responds negatively in a conversation, helplessly wondering, *What did I say?* Combine this with the difficulty many men have articulating their feelings (i.e., *why* they are upset), and you've got a combustible—and frustrating—situation.

A disrespect barometer

So how do we know when we've crossed the disrespect line? Thankfully, there is one easy barometer: Check for anger.

Before I elaborate, let me ask you to consider a question: If you are in a conflict with the man in your life, do you think that it is legitimate to break down and cry? Most of us would probably answer yes. Let me ask another question: In that same conflict, do you think it is legitimate for your man to get really angry? Many of us have a problem with that—we think he's not controlling himself or that he's behaving improperly.

But Dr. Emerson Eggerichs, founder of Love and Respect Ministries, has an entirely different interpretation: "In a relationship conflict, crying is often a woman's response to feeling unloved, and anger is often a man's response to feeling disrespected."

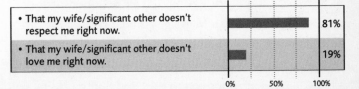 Anger is often a man's response to feeling disrespected.

If a man can't articulate his feelings in the heat of the moment, he won't necessarily blurt out something helpful like "You're disrespecting me!" But rest assured, if he's angry at something you've said or done and you don't understand the cause, there is a good chance that he is feeling the pain or humiliation of your disrespect.

If you want confirmation of this, consider the extremely telling response from the survey. More than *80 percent* of men—four out of five—said that in a conflict they were likely to be feeling disrespected. Whereas we girls are far more likely to be wailing, "He doesn't love me!"

Even the best relationships sometimes have conflicts on day-to-day issues. In the middle of a conflict with my wife/significant other, I am more likely to be feeling... [Choose One Answer]

• That my wife/significant other doesn't respect me right now.	81%
• That my wife/significant other doesn't love me right now.	19%

0%   50%   100%

"Unconditional respect"

Just as you want the man in your life to love you uncondi-tionally, even when you're not particularly lovable, your man needs you to demonstrate your respect for him regard-less of whether he's meeting your expectations at the moment.

"We've become such a love-dominated culture," Dr. Eggerichs says. "Like the Beatles said, 'All you need is love.' So we've come to think that love should be unconditional, but respect must be earned. Instead, what men need is *unconditional respect*—to be respected for who they are [i.e., our husbands], apart from how they do."

Notice that one of the main biblical passages on mar-riage—in Ephesians 5—never tells the wife to love her husband, and it never tells the husband to respect his wife (presumably because we each already tend to give what we want to receive). Instead, over and over, it urges the hus-band to *love* his wife and urges the wife to *respect* her husband and his leadership. Women often tend to want to control things, which, unfortunately, men tend to interpret as disrespect and distrust (which, if we're honest with our-selves, it sometimes *is*). Marriage is about putting the other person's needs above your own (he's required to do that too, remember), and it does tremendous things for your man to know that you are choosing to trust and honor him.

It's a choice!

And that reveals the most important aspect of demonstrating respect: It is a choice. A choice that we make out of reverence for God and love for our husbands.

> Just as our men can choose to demonstrate love toward us even if they don't feel it at the moment, we can and should choose to demonstrate respect.

Just as our men can *choose* to demonstrate love toward us even if they don't feel it at the moment, we can and should choose to demonstrate respect toward them. In fact, the Greek word translated as "respect" in Ephesians, *phobeo*, means to be in awe of, to revere. It's not just a matter of bland regard. We are supposed to be highly valuing our men!*

IT'S NOT REAL UNLESS YOU *SHOW* IT

You wouldn't believe the number of men who told me that they know, deep down, that their mate respects and values them, but that she doesn't necessarily show it. My own husband put it this way: "Deep down, I don't really doubt that you respect me. I'm frustrated sometimes that you don't know *how* to respect me, that you don't know what is affirming to me as a man."

Feeling respect for our husbands but not overtly showing it is the same as their feeling love for us but not showing it! It's like that awful joke: "Why do I have to tell my wife I love her? I told her that when we got married!" Just as a wife would feel dreadful if her husband never demonstrated his love, a husband feels dreadful if a wife never demonstrates her respect. It's not a negotiable!

> The way a man needs to feel your respect is quite different from the way you need to feel his love.

However, the way a man needs to feel your respect is quite different from the way you need to feel his love. Most women appreciate it when a husband says, "I love you." But, as I discovered pretty quickly, it just doesn't do it for a guy to hear his wife coo, "Oh, honey, I respect you *so* much." He *does* need to hear, "Honey, I'm so proud of you," and "I trust you." But beyond that, demonstrating respect, day in and day out, means far more than just saying a few words.

How do you do that? The men's comments tended to fall into one of four key needs.

Need #1: Respect his judgment.

The men were really touchy about this. A man deeply needs the woman in his life to respect his knowledge, opinions, and decisions—what I would call his judgment. No one wanted a silent wallflower (nor would I advocate that!), but many men wished their mate wouldn't question their knowledge or argue with their decisions all the time. It's a touchy (and difficult) thing in these liberated days, but what it really comes down to is their need for us to defer to them sometimes.

I can easily show respect on the positive side—for example, I can demonstrate that I respect Jeff by calling on his knowledge in a given subject. But sometimes it is a lot harder for me not to show disrespect! It takes a lot more effort for me to defer to Jeff's judgment when I want to seize control of a matter or want to prove that I'm right. I'll argue an issue (and my husband) into the ground!

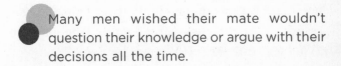

Many men wished their mate wouldn't question their knowledge or argue with their decisions all the time.

Several men confessed that they felt like their opinions and decisions were actively valued in every area of their lives *except* at home. Some men felt that their comrades at work trusted their judgment more than their own wives did.

Also, while a man's partners or colleagues will rarely tell him what to do (they ask him or collaborate on the decision instead), more than one wife has made the mistake of ordering her husband around like one of the kids.

Early in my marriage, sad to say, I unconsciously made that mistake far too many times. Jeff finally told me how stupid it made him feel, and hearing that was enough to shake me of my habit. On the surveys, many men said the one thing they wished they could tell their wives was to "show more trust in my decision-making abilities"—which is code for (among other things) "I'm not stupid."

Need #2: Respect his abilities.

Another strong theme that emerged was that men want—even *need*—to figure things out for themselves. And if they can, they feel like they have conquered something and are affirmed as men. For some reason, spending hours figuring out how to put together the new DVD player is fun. Problem is, we want to help them—and guess how they interpret that? You got it: distrust. (It's a wonder *any* relationships work and that the human race didn't die out millennia ago!)

And, of course, our attention is not all benign. Sometimes we truly *don't* have confidence that our man can figure something out on his own. On the survey, one man wished he could tell his wife, "Trust in my judgment on everyday items. Have confidence in my general abilities of learning, application, fixing, rebuilding, repair, etc., without having to do it your way because you know it and think I do not."

> Problem is, we want to help them—and guess how they interpret that? You got it: distrust.

Honey, will you please just ask...?

It turns out that the old joke about men never wanting to stop and ask for directions is based on this truth—that men love figuring things out for themselves. If they can find their way through the hazards of the concrete jungle with only a tattered map and their wits, they feel like they've conquered something. They feel affirmed, excited, encouraged, alive.

Realizing that, now put yourself in your man's shoes and listen to this phrase: "Honey, can we please just stop and ask for directions?" He's out to conquer Everest, and you're telling him you don't believe he can do it. And remember how important it is to a guy that his mate believes in him! When you tell him to ask for directions, you're telling him point-blank that you don't trust him to figure it out for himself.

Now, if you're like me, you're probably saying to yourself, "You're right, I don't trust him! How on earth could he know how to find the highway entrance in this maze of streets?"

Well, there you have it, don't you? Are you going to decide to trust him or not? This particular "will I trust him" question is just a metaphor for all the little trust choices we make. Having talked to dozens of men about this representative subject, here is their near-unanimous opinion: Let him do it. As several men said, "I'm not an idiot, okay? If I didn't think I could find what I was looking for, why would I be trying?"

Another said, "You're right. I may have no idea where I'm going. But it's fun, it's a challenge, to try to find my own way. And I'm not stupid—I've got a clock on the dashboard. I know whether we're going to be late or not."

The little things equal one big clue

We don't realize that the act of *forcing* ourselves to trust our men in these little things means so much to them, but it does. It's not a big deal to us, so we don't get that it's a big deal to them. We don't get that our responses to these little choices to trust or not trust—or at least act like we do!—are interpreted as signs of our overall trust and respect for them as men.

A man might think of it like this: *If she doesn't trust me in something as small as finding my way along a road, why would she trust me in something important, like being a good breadwinner or a good father? If she doesn't respect me in this small thing, she probably doesn't really respect me at all.*

The next time your husband stubbornly drives in circles, ask yourself what is more important: being on time to the party or his feeling trusted. No contest.

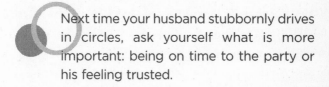

Next time your husband stubbornly drives in circles, ask yourself what is more important: being on time to the party or his feeling trusted.

Don't tell him how

The movie *The Natural* provides a powerful example of a woman's respect for a man. Robert Redford plays an amazing baseball talent who, after mysteriously leaving his girlfriend and dropping out of sight for years, has finally gotten to the major leagues. After taking the world by storm, he suddenly hits a humiliating slump and starts doubting himself. In this powerful scene, his old flame watches from the stands as he strikes out again and again. When the dispirited Redford comes up for his final at-bat, to scattered boos from the crowd, she suddenly stands up, alone, in the stands. Somehow he senses her presence, awakes from his slumber, and slams a home run, reigniting his passion and his game.

One man, explaining why he loves that scene, said, "She just stood up and supported him. She didn't come down from the stands and tell him what to do or how to fix what was wrong. She didn't tell him how to hold his bat. She just supported him and let *him* figure it out."

Another man agreed. "She stood up and publicly said, 'I know you can do it.' For any man, especially if he is in a season of self-doubt, that is *exactly* what he needs to be able to hit a home run in life."

> "She stood up and publicly said, 'I know you can do it.' For any man, that is exactly what he needs to be able to hit a home run."

Ladies, it is so easy for us to bristle at this idea and say, "Why *can't* I tell him how to hold his bat? We're equal partners! What if I know how better than he does?"

Well, of course you *can* tell him. Most of us are perfectly competent to advise our men in all sorts of areas. But remember, *he's* the one up to bat, with his feeling of competency on the line. True advice usually isn't a problem. But advice can quickly become instruction, and there we are, again, trying to get in the batter's box and do it for him, implying that he can't do it himself.

But what if you don't want to stand up for your man? What if he has so disappointed you that you feel that supporting him would just condone his mistakes? As another man pointed out, "That movie scene is a powerful illustration of what can happen when a woman chooses to honor and respect her man publicly, even when he may not deserve it. Instead of that choice somehow being demeaning or unfair to her, her act of showing respect lifted them both up."

Need #3: Respect in communication.

Women hold an incredible power in the way we communicate with our men (both husbands and sons) to build them up or to tear them down, to encourage or to exasperate.

Some things just push a man's buttons. This goes beyond *what* we say—such as questioning a man's judgment or his abilities—and into *how* we say it (and *where* we say it, which is the subject of the next section).

The disconnect

In my interviews, a large number of men said something like this: "When my wife says something disrespectful, I often think, *I can't believe she doesn't know how that makes me feel!*" I had to reassure these men over and over that their wives probably didn't *mean* to disrespect them and were likely just clueless.

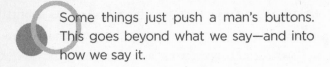

Some things just push a man's buttons. This goes beyond what we say—and into how we say it.

Let me give you several common examples of how a man might hear something negative where the woman never intended it.

Hearing disrespect

Not long ago, I was asking Jeff and one of his married colleagues about the dynamic of men wanting to do things for themselves. This man said, "Sometimes, if something breaks in the house, I want to try to take a crack at it before I call an expert. If my wife says, 'Well, you're really not a fix-it–type person,' I feel so insulted. She's not rude about it or anything, but it's like she doesn't respect me enough to believe that I can figure it out if I put my mind to it, even if it takes me a while."

This man's wife is one of my closest friends, and I know that she respects her husband and would never intentionally disparage him. So it was eye-opening to hear that what was (to her) an offhand remark was something he took extremely seriously—and, if I may delicately say so, extremely *wrong*.

Hearing disappointment

In the survey—as in life—a sizable minority of men read something negative into a simple female reminder. I asked men what would go through their minds if their wife or significant other reminded them that the kitchen wall was damaged and it still had to be fixed. More than one-third of these men took that reminder as nagging or as an accusation of laziness or mistrust.

Several months ago, I met with my friend and book agent Calvin Edwards at Starbucks to start designing the original survey questions. When we saw a local pastor Calvin knew, I ran the "kitchen wall" question by him and asked what would go through his mind. Consider his illuminating response:

> *Pastor:* "I'm irritated because I have to be reminded. I hate being reminded."
>
> *Calvin:* "Why is that a problem? Look at your Day Planner there—you set up systems to remind yourself of things all the time."
>
> *Pastor:* "Inherent in her reminder is a statement of disappointment. For me as a man, that is saying

that I failed. I hate to fail. It's not <u>the statement that</u> <u>bothers me; it's the implications of the statement."</u>

Now, another interesting thing about the survey results was that those who jumped to negative conclusions were still in the minority. A larger group—fully half of the men polled—simply didn't place as high a priority on the task as the wife did and said it would get done eventually.

Hearing attacks

I got an excellent example of how our words can be misinterpreted as an attack when Chuck Cowan and I were discussing a survey question I had drafted: "Do you know how to put together a romantic event that your partner would enjoy?"

> *Chuck:* "That question won't work because you're starting off in attack mode."
>
> *Me:* "Huh?"
>
> *Chuck:* "You're starting off suggesting the man is inept."
>
> *Me* (thinking to myself): *Suggesting the man is inept? What is he talking about?*
>
> *Chuck:* "Soften it a bit—put it into a context that isn't so blatant."

Simply by adding a context sentence to the beginning—
"Suppose you had to plan an anniversary event for your
partner. Do you know how…?"—the question was deemed
totally appropriate not to step on male toes or question a
man's adequacy.

Apparently, the difference is all about softening our
approach!

Crank up that filtering system

No matter what *we* think we are saying, in the end, what
matters is what the guy is hearing. Obviously, some people
can be overly sensitive, and we can't walk on eggshells all
the time. Nor do we want to pass up all opportunities to help
them understand *our* communication wiring.

> No matter what we think we are saying, in the
> end, what matters is what the guy is hearing.

That said, considering that most men appear to be
highly sensitive to disrespect—including seeing disrespect
where none is intended—I would argue that it is not the
average man who needs to be less sensitive to a woman's
words, but the average woman who needs to be more sensitive to her man's feelings.

After all, don't we want our husbands to adjust to *our* sensitivities? Do you want your husband to publicly tease you about gaining ten pounds? It's all about loving each other the way the other person needs to be loved. Even as we help our husbands understand that we have a learning curve on this, we should make every effort to filter our words through a "disrespect meter" before they pass our lips.

Need #4: Respect in public.

Now we come to one of the most important points of the book. There appears to be an epidemic of public disrespect for men, and the biggest culprit is not television, movies, or other media, but the women who are supposed to love their men most.

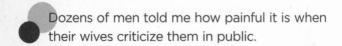

Dozens of men told me how painful it is when their wives criticize them in public.

"The most fragile thing on the planet"

Dozens of men told me how painful it is when their wives criticize them in public, put them down, or even question their judgment in front of others. One man on the survey said that the one thing he wished he could tell his wife was that "at a minimum, she should be supportive of me in public." That wish was repeated dozens of times on the survey—it was one of the strongest themes that emerged.

Consider this statement, which I have heard (in essence) from many men: "My wife says things about me in public that she considers teasing. I consider them torture."

One married man put it very starkly: "The male ego is the most fragile thing on the planet. Women have this thought that *He's got such a huge ego that I need to take him down a peg.* No way. The male ego is incredibly fragile."

We women often think of this as male pride—but that isn't it. What is at stake isn't his pride as much as his secret feelings of inadequacy as a man. There's a big difference between feeling prideful and feeling adequate. What happens in public isn't that his "inflated" pride is brought down to ground level, but that something made him feel inadequate and humiliated as a man.

Teasing can be torture

Even good-natured teasing can sometimes be humiliating, not to mention more pointed jabs. Many of us have wondered why our men—who normally have a great sense of humor—get so upset by a little public joking at their expense. I was writing this chapter at my computer one day over the holidays, and my parents were around. I asked my dad a question, and my husband came into the office as we were talking. The resulting discussion was so fascinating—

and foundational—that I started typing it into my file. Here is a portion:

> *Me:* "What *sort* of teasing might a man take wrong?"
>
> *Dad:* "Anything that seems to show that the man is not somehow in control or not getting respect from his wife. A man would never take that from another man unless he wanted a fight."
>
> *Me:* "But what if she's truly teasing? Like they're out with friends, and the wife says, 'Oh, the dishwasher broke,' and she teases her husband about wanting to fix it when he's not a handyman?"
>
> *Dad:* "Oh, that's terrible. You never want to do that. The guy is the protector, provider, and is supposed to take care of everything. This sort of teasing lets everyone know that he doesn't know how to take care of everything. It also lets everyone know how the *wife* feels about him—she's making light of something that is really important to him! But if a guy feels that he ought to be able to do something as the provider and he *can't,* he *never* makes light of it in his heart."
>
> *Jeff:* "It all depends on whether that particular guy already feels inadequate in that area. That same thing may not hit another man wrong."

Me: "Does it make a difference if the wife is teasing him in front of men or women?"

Dad: "Oh, it's much worse in front of men. After an incident early on in our marriage, I asked your mom, 'Please, don't *ever* embarrass me in front of another man.'"

Me: "Why?"

Dad: "Guys are always in competition with each other. Your wife is the person who knows you better than anyone, and if *she* doesn't respect you, how can you expect another man to?"

Jeff: "It's also humiliating to know that the other guy feels sorry for me because my wife doesn't respect me."

Dad: "Even worse, if the other man doesn't know you well, it is a sign of weakness. The other man is thinking, *If this guy's own wife doesn't respect him, he's nothing. We'll run him over the next time we do a deal together.* If you belittle your husband in front of another man, you can even ruin his career. I'm not kidding. Because any man he works with will now see him as weak."

Me: "Back to the teasing question…"

Dad: "You have to understand—men don't let down their guard easily. They don't let down their guard with other men unless they are very close. Most men probably crave a situation where they can, but they aren't naturally made that way—its all a competition instead. The only time a guy's guard is completely down is with the woman he loves. So she can pierce his heart like no one else."

"The only time a guy's guard is completely down is with the woman he loves. So she can pierce his heart like no one else."

Be respectful even when he's absent

Having seen how important public respect is to men (it is almost impossible to overstate), I have become incredibly sensitive to how often we might talk negatively about them behind their backs. The effects are much the same even when a man isn't present: The woman's disrespect of her husband becomes even more deeply embedded as she harps on it, and those in listening range may begin to feel the same! I have a dear friend who loves and is so proud of her husband, but for some reason she also regularly complains about him. I'm convinced that's one of the main reasons she can't shake a nagging dissatisfaction with their relationship—a dissatisfaction that then affects him.

Ladies, let's kill this terrible habit!

Showing public respect goes a long way

Just as your man will be hurt and angry if you disrespect him in public, he will think you are the most wonderful woman in the world if you publicly build him up. This is not artificial. It simply means taking those little opportunities to *honestly* praise him or to ask his opinion in front of others. Do you think he's a great father? Tell your dinner guests a story about something he did with the kids yesterday that proves it. Are you impressed with his baseball ability? Brag on his great game last weekend. Did he take the kids out and let you sleep in Saturday morning? Tell your book club and make the other girls jealous.

Trust me—from the men I've talked to, that will be the equivalent of his coming home to you with a dozen roses and a surprise date night without the kids. He will feel *adored*.

Need #5: Respect in our assumptions.

Unfortunately, in one area men have every right to read something into what we say—and that is when we have jumped to negative conclusions about them. When we really examine our communication, we'll be astounded at how often it assumes something *bad* about the man we love. See if any of these assumptions ring a bell.

We assume, "He needs to be reminded"

To us, repeatedly asking "Have you done it yet?" is probably not a big deal. But inherent in the question is our assumption that the guy *needs* the reminder—that he is either incapable of remembering on his own or that he remembers just fine but needs our prodding to do the job. It's no wonder many men hate being nagged. What they are accurately hearing is "I don't trust you."

Instead, what if we were to proactively assume the best of him instead of the worst? For example: "I asked him to do it. He hasn't done it. I trust my husband. Therefore, there's a *reason* he hasn't done it."

Just realize that his reason for not doing it may be different from yours—which makes it no less legitimate. Remember, half the men on the survey indicated that sometimes they just have different priorities. Or they could just be unable to handle one more thing. One man with a stressful job noted that he sometimes feels like a computer that will crash if he tries to load one more thing onto it. For him, procrastinating on something his wife wants him to do at home is his warning sign that he will emotionally (or even physically) crash if he tries it.

Remember the "kitchen wall" question I posed to the pastor at Starbucks? Here's how he put it:

I've revealed something about my preferences and priorities by *not* fixing it for a week. If I come home with the world on my shoulders—if a couple at church is divorcing or I'm worried that a key employee might leave—and my wife is in her house mode and says the living room fern is dying, that is hard for me to engage in. The brutal truth is that it's not as important to me. My response is, "Get a fern doctor." But Scripture says that as a husband I have to lay down my life for my wife, so sometimes I have to talk about the fern. But we have a little code now, where I'll tell her it's "fern doctor stuff" to let her know that sometimes my brain just doesn't go there.

Procrastinating on a home task can be a sign that he's about to emotionally or physically crash.

We assume, "He's choosing not to help"

One experienced female marriage counselor gave me this example: "If my husband doesn't help with the kids or the cleaning, I shouldn't assume that he sees it and is choosing not to help. I should start with the assumption that he doesn't see it."

Unfortunately, because that dynamic is spot-on in my household (but in reverse—I'm the one who doesn't "see" the clutter or the laundry), I can attest to how frustrating that assumption is and how grateful I am when Jeff gives me the benefit of the doubt and asks for help.

We assume, "It's because of him"

Finally (and I know this is a shocking thought), sometimes something is not his fault—*it's ours.* Sometimes we assign unloving motives to our men that could actually be traced back to something we have inadvertently said or done. For example, a wife who is constantly critical of her husband may spur him to withdraw emotionally to protect himself, thereby becoming unloving where he wasn't before.

"Men are not stupid," says Dr. Eggerichs. "They are not Neanderthals. Sometimes these behaviors that appear to be unloving are not unloving at all. They are reacting that way because they interpret something as disrespect. Even if sometimes they shouldn't."

SO WHAT SHOULD WE DO?

We as women hold incredible power—and responsibility— in our hands. We have the ability to either build up or tear down our men. We can either strengthen or hobble them in ways that go far beyond our relationship because respect at home affects every area of a man's life. There is something unique in how a man approaches the world that makes his inner, home-fired feelings of personal adequacy absolutely foundational to everything else.

So what should we do? As one man powerfully put it, "Always assume the best and you will find it easier to show respect." Simple as it sounds, from now on we can choose to demonstrate respect and choose *not* to demonstrate disrespect, starting with never humiliating them in public. (Again, how would we like it if he "joked" to everyone that we had gained ten pounds?)

We can take every opportunity, in public and private, to demonstrate—by words and actions—how proud we are of our men and how much we trust them. Just as we love to hear "I love you," a man's heart is powerfully touched by a few simple words: "I'm so proud of you."

A man's heart is powerfully touched by a few simple words: "I'm so proud of you."

And when we realize that we've blown it, we can acknowledge our fault and ask for forgiveness. While we might be tempted to push and prod, several men recommended otherwise. As one man advised, *"Don't say, 'I'm sorry I made you feel XYZ.'* Men don't want to be told how they are feeling! And honestly, sometimes we don't even *know* how we're feeling, so it's better to let us process it for a while." Instead the men recommended saying something like, "I'm sorry I did that—that was disrespectful. I know I can trust you."

It's not just for them, but for us

Consider this man's plea: "She has to make me feel respected so that I can command respect out in the world. If she defeats me emotionally, I can't win the race and bring home the prize for her."

> If a man's wife believes in him, he can conquer the world—or at least his little corner of it.

Another man told me, "You know that saying 'Behind every good man is a great woman?' Well, that is *so true*. If a man's wife is supportive and believes in him, he can conquer the world—or at least his little corner of it. He will do better at work, at home, everywhere. By contrast, very few men can do well at work *or* at home if their wives make them feel inadequate."

As you now have glimpsed, inside their confident exterior many men are very vulnerable and even insecure. That is the subject of the next chapter.

*For the purpose of this book, I'm assuming that we love and respect our men, even if we encounter problems in our relationship. But I recognize that some readers may no longer respect or value the man in their lives, and I urge you to explore the many resources available to help you and your marriage (some are listed at www.4-womenonly.com).

But also recognize three things: First, that you may be caught in what Emerson Eggerichs dubs the "crazy cycle"—the unfortunate dynamic where your man doesn't give enough love, so you don't give enough respect, so he feels slighted and doesn't give enough love...and on and on. Second, recognize that feelings often *follow* words or actions, not the other way around. For example, if you regularly disparage your husband to him or to your friends, it shouldn't be surprising that you feel contempt. And that leads to the third point, which is that we can choose to honor and demonstrate respect to our husbands even if we have a relationship that makes that choice difficult. I have seen many lives and relationships changed by such a one-sided choice!

Chapter 3

THE PERFORMANCE OF A LIFETIME

Why Your Mr. Smooth Looks So Impressive but Feels Like an Impostor

Despite their "in control" exterior, men often feel like impostors and are insecure that their inadequacies will be discovered.

At the risk of admitting that I am a closet Trekkie (hey, everyone has their weakness), let me take you to an old episode of *Star Trek: The Next Generation*. The confident captain, Jean-Luc Picard, and his friend Dr. Beverly Crusher are (of course) stuck on a dangerous and unfamiliar planet. And their predicament has an interesting twist: Because of some unwanted alien meddling, the two can hear each other's thoughts.

As the captain leads them toward help, he scans the

unfamiliar horizon, motions in a particular direction, and says, with his usual commanding certainty, "This way."

Since she can hear what he is actually thinking, the doctor stares at him and says, "You don't really know, do you? You're acting like you know exactly which way to go, but you're only guessing!" Then, with growing amazement, she asks, "Do you do this all the time?"

He gives her a look, then answers. "There are times when it is necessary for a captain to give the appearance of confidence."

> Dr. Crusher had just discovered what most of us never grasp—that your man is hiding a deep inner uncertainty.

In this chapter I want to take you inside your man's head and show you what he is really thinking and feeling. You see, Dr. Crusher had just discovered what most of us never grasp—that your man is hiding a deep inner uncertainty.

This inner uncertainty leaves even the most confident-seeming man dreading the moment when he will be exposed for who he really is—or at least believes himself to be.

An impostor.

"THEY ARE GOING TO FIND ME OUT!"

A man's inner vulnerability about his performance often stems from his conviction that at all times he is being watched and judged. In my follow-up survey, I found that no matter how secure the men looked on the outside, two-thirds admitted being insecure about others' opinion of them.

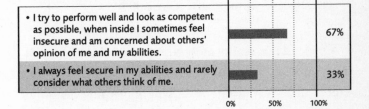

Regardless of how successful you are in your current job, which statement most closely describes your feelings about your work life? [Choose One Answer]

• I try to perform well and look as competent as possible, when inside I sometimes feel insecure and am concerned about others' opinion of me and my abilities.	67%
• I always feel secure in my abilities and rarely consider what others think of me.	33%

0%   50%   100%

This secret male vulnerability involves not just a concern about what others think of them, but also the internal realization that since they *don't* always know what they are doing, they are just one mess-up away from being found out.

In fact, when doing something new or unfamiliar—a common situation—more than *four out of five* men are insecure, but don't want it to show. Only a small fraction expressed confidence in their ability to handle the task.

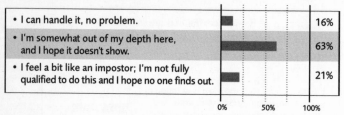

Men who are taking risks and progressing in their careers will inevitably face many situations that are somewhat unfamiliar and challenging. Think back over several situations like that in your career. Which one of these feelings were you most likely to experience? [Choose One Answer]

• I can handle it, no problem.	16%
• I'm somewhat out of my depth here, and I hope it doesn't show.	63%
• I feel a bit like an impostor; I'm not fully qualified to do this and I hope no one finds out.	21%

Obviously, in reality most bosses or colleagues are relatively tolerant of mistakes and would probably even expect them if someone was doing something new—but logic appears to have very little to do with how men feel about this.

To compensate for his insecurity—and his feeling of being watched—a man may feel the need to work long hours. Or he may get emotionally worn down by the constant need to look "on the ball."

One thing is certain: *The idea of someone thinking he can't cut it is humiliating—a feeling every man wants to avoid at all costs.* So he puts up a good front so others will think he's highly competent. And there we are, back at the beginning. In the spotlight stands a man—maybe your husband—feeling sure that if anyone (even his wife) really knew him for what he was, they'd know the truth. The truth that—at least some of the time—he is not what he appears to be.

> The idea of someone thinking he can't cut it is humiliating—a feeling every man wants to avoid at all costs.

WHAT'S DRIVING HIM?

As I began to understand this, I was saddened to realize that I had sometimes not been very supportive, simply because I didn't realize that my husband could possibly be feeling insecure. I'm fully confident in Jeff's abilities, after all—why wouldn't he be?

Just so we can recognize it when we see it, here are several things that seem to drive this part of our men's inner lives.

"I'm always being judged"

Men told me they are hard enough on themselves without any external pressure. Add in the conviction that the eyes of the world are critically trained on them, and you suddenly see how uncomfortable and insecure they might feel. One man put it this way: "We think about what others think about us *all the time*."

One male friend shared an amusing anecdote that perfectly captured this myopic male certainty:

When I was in college, I drove one of the school transit buses part-time to earn money. Sometimes, when I had no one on board, I drove—um—rather quickly. One day I came hurtling around a corner, and there was an elderly man standing at the bus stop, shaking his head no at me. It irritated me that he was disapproving of my driving! Years later I lived in New York City, and one day I shook my head no to tell an approaching bus driver not to stop because I didn't need his particular route. Suddenly, it hit me: All those years ago that elderly man had just been saying no, he didn't need my route. Instead, I built up this whole assumption that he had examined my performance and found me wanting. That is a silly example, but it's what every guy does.

This man went on to clarify, "It's your abilities *and* you that are being judged. Men aren't always as sure of themselves as they look. That's why when your wife makes a joke at your expense in front of other people, it's a knife."

"I have no earthly idea how to do this"

Another male friend illustrated the "impostor complex" with a recent story:

> A young friend of mine had just gotten a job as a college professor. He had never done these particular lesson plans, so he was running to stay one step ahead of his students. Often, he would literally be one day ahead of them in the textbook. One evening, one of his students ran into him on campus and said she was looking forward to his class in the morning. She said, "I wish I knew as much as you do about this stuff." He smiled and nodded, but inside he was thinking, *Tomorrow, you will!*

My friend said, "*That* is a perfect description of how many men feel as they go through life, especially whenever they do something unfamiliar—*which most of us have to do all the time.* A client may be asking me to do something new, and I may be smiling and nodding, but in the back of my mind I'm thinking, *I have no earthly idea how to do this, and I hope I can learn it before they find out.*"

What was startling about this conversation is that I have worked with this man for years, and he is an extremely competent businessman. I had originally thought that maybe this dynamic only affected younger, less-experienced men. But hearing the same thing from those who are highly accomplished helped me realize just how deep-seated this vulnerability is.

"But I *want* to do this!"

The inner insecurity I've described has an interesting partner—the feeling of wanting a challenge, wanting to take on something new and exciting. These two feelings may seem contradictory, but they are all part of the male package. Men want to conquer Everest (or at the very least, the mean streets of the city), but they also know they'll have to risk taking a humiliating tumble on the way.

One man put it this way:

> When a guy does something that he's never done before and he's being paid for it, he thinks, *I can do this, but what if they find out this is my first time?* There's a joke among some guys that you're going to be talking in front of a group sometime, and your fourth-grade teacher's going to run in and say, "He doesn't know what he's talking about! He was a D

student!" It's this irrational, debilitating fear that you'll publicly be found out. And sooner or later, every man has to face it. Because if you want to move up, that will inevitably mean doing something new.

As you might guess, those times are when men feel the shakiest and need the most encouragement from us.

THE IMPOSTOR AT WORK

As you'd expect, a man's uncertainty about his adequacy usually takes its greatest toll on the job. One man put it this way. "We have incredible anxiety over where we stand at work. I start to think that the fact that my boss isn't communicating with me means that he's found me out. This creates intense anxiety and uncertainty."

> A man's uncertainty about his adequacy usually takes its greatest toll on the job.

"I want to see you first thing Monday morning..."
Frank Maguire helped start Federal Express and earlier held an inside position in the Kennedy White House. He

takes us inside the unique torture of a man's workplace anxiety in his book *You're the Greatest*.

Every Friday as he left the FedEx office, Maguire called his good-byes to FedEx founder Fred Smith, and Fred would call back, "Thanks for going the extra mile this week."

Maguire always left with a bounce in his step. Then came the Friday when his cheery good-bye was met by silence, and then, "Frank, I want to see you first thing Monday morning."

"I had a lousy weekend," Maguire says. "Not only me, but my wife, my kids, even Thor, the wonder dog. We all had a miserable weekend."

On Monday, when he nervously asked Fred, "What did you want to talk to me about?" he was met with a puzzled look. "Oh, I forget. It wasn't important."

You can guess why Frank Maguire had a miserable weekend—he was expecting to be fired. But why would he think that? He was a successful, valued executive at a fast-growing business. He had even been trusted by the President of the United States. So why did he assume a "neutral" comment was a portent of woe?

Because inside he felt like an impostor. And he was sure he had just been found out.

Maguire writes: "I've been around many powerful leaders. On the surface, they looked totally secure. You would never guess there was even one ounce of fear. But my experience has also convinced me that no matter what your title or position in life is, we all, no exceptions, carry our treasures in fragile containers."

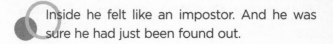

Inside he felt like an impostor. And he was sure he had just been found out.

"We're all on the replacement list"

One of the most revealing interviews I conducted was with Ken Ruettgers, a former All-Pro offensive tackle with the Superbowl-champ Green Bay Packers. He now helps retiring athletes make the difficult transition into well-balanced, regular lives.

When I told him the subject of this chapter, he jumped on it. "I've never seen so many insecurities as in the locker room," he said. Surprised, I asked him why. Here's his explanation:

> Because the guys are naked on the field. They have two or three hours to prove themselves, and there's no fooling the camera. Once you look through the mask, you've got the most insecure guys ever. They try to put up a great front, but once they know each

other really well, they'll ask, "How'd I do on that play?" They are just *looking* for affirmation.

And it's not just the camera—it's the knowledge that some guys are going to get cut. [Another All-Pro football player] put it this way: "We're all on the replacement list. You just want to stay off the top of it."

You know, sports is like corporate America—there's a "what have you done for me lately" attitude. It's incredibly draining and there is a huge, unspoken fear of failure.

Ken went on to make an important note about how that fear can be used. "Keep in mind that guys can use that fear of failure for good. It gets you out of bed in the morning. It gets you to the gym when you wouldn't go otherwise."

Ken's words helped me realize why so many men—talented, effective men—work such long hours. Sometimes the long hours are a necessity for the job. But not always. Sometimes they are (in the guy's mind) an insurance against fear—fear of falling behind, fear of being cut from the team.

THE IMPOSTOR AT HOME

The male sense of performance anxiety doesn't, as one man put it, "just end when we walk through the front door." Many men feel just as inadequate at home.

The majority of men *do* want to be good husbands. But in the same way they worry that they may not know everything about being a good employee, they secretly worry that they don't know how to succeed at being a good husband, father, provider, or handyman.

"At least at work," one man told me, "I have an idea of how to succeed—work hard, get ahead, complete assignments, and get in good with the boss. At home, what is the measure of success? How do I know whether I am a success or a failure?"

Not surprisingly, men said they judge themselves—and feel that others judge them—based on the happiness and respect of their wives.

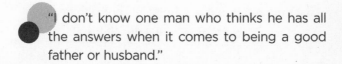

"I don't know one man who thinks he has all the answers when it comes to being a good father or husband."

If a man feels like he's trying to bluff his way through this being-a-husband thing, you can imagine his relief when he can tell that his wife feels loved and happy, or when she publicly honors him and his "husbanding abilities." And conversely, you can imagine the trepidation he feels when he receives the cold shoulder confirmation that he got it wrong again, that he is indeed an impostor, that he doesn't know what he's doing in his personal life.

One man wrote me a note about this:

> I don't know one man who thinks he has all the answers when it comes to being a good father or husband. If we've had good fathers, then we try and remember what our father would do in the situation. If we didn't have good fathers, we feel like we're making it up as we go. If my wife often challenges my decisions or appears displeased with me as a husband—it's the impostor all over again. It may even cause a man to withdraw from taking an active role in the lives of his wife and kids if he doesn't think he can do it well or be affirmed in it. That's not a rational or Christlike approach by the man, for sure, but that is how some guys feel.

WHAT SHOULD WE DO?

So what on earth should we do about this? It's not your man's responsibility to figure all this out on his own. Once we understand what our husbands secretly feel and think, our words and actions can make a huge difference.

Affirm him!

"Affirmation is everything"

Have you ever noticed how the adulterous woman in the book of Proverbs seduces the unwitting young man? It's not with sex (okay, not *just* with sex); it's with flattery. "She threw her arms around him...and with a brazen look she said, 'I've offered my sacrifices and just finished my vows. It's you I was looking for!'... With her flattery she enticed him. He followed her at once" (from Proverbs 7).

Flattery is simply a seductive counterfeit for affirmation. As one marriage counselor told me, "Affirmation is everything. When a man is affirmed, he can conquer the world. When he's not, he is sapped of his confidence and even his feeling of manhood. And believe me, he *will*, consciously or unconsciously, seek out places where he receives affirmation."

Home is the most important place for a man to be affirmed. If a man knows that his wife believes in him, he is empowered to do better in every area of his life. A man tends to think of life as a competition and a battle, and he can energetically go duke it out if he can come home to someone who supports him unconditionally, who will wipe his brow and tell him he can do it. As one of our close friends told me, "It's all about whether my wife thinks I can do it. A husband can slay dragons, climb mountains, and win great victories if *he* believes his *wife* believes that he can."

Don't tear him down!

If instead of affirming, a wife reinforces her husband's feelings of inadequacy, it can become a self-fulfilling prophecy. For example, if we focus our attention on what he is doing *wrong* in the relationship, we can unwittingly undermine what we most want—for him to do it *right*.

Of the men I surveyed, only one man in four felt actively appreciated by his family.

But I discovered a dismaying fact. Of the men I surveyed, only one man in four felt actively appreciated by his family. And 44 percent of men actually felt *unappreciated* at home. More pointedly, men in their prime years of responsibility for home, children, and work—men between the ages of thirty-six and fifty-five—felt even less appreciated.

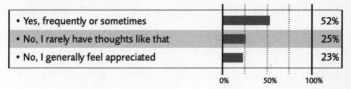

In your **home life**, do you have thoughts like **I'm not appreciated around here?** [Choose One Answer] *Men ages thirty-six to fifty-five:*

• Yes, frequently or sometimes	52%
• No, I rarely have thoughts like that	25%
• No, I generally feel appreciated	23%

0%   50%   100%

I'll bet that many of the wives or girlfriends of these men would be surprised to learn that they didn't feel appreciated. My guess is that most of us *do* appreciate our men but don't show it enough.

He'll seek affirmation somewhere

If a man isn't convinced that his woman thinks he's the greatest, he will tend to seek affirmation elsewhere. He may spend more hours at work, where he feels alive and on top of his game, or he may spend too much time talking to the admiring female associate. He may immerse himself in watching or playing sports, feeling the thrill of the competitive rush. Or he may retreat to his workshop or his home office, feeling like he can control things there even if he feels inadequate and clumsy elsewhere.

"Why else do you think," one man asked me, "so many men take sports so seriously? It's something they feel good at, something they've practiced. They are admired and encouraged by other men on the field. People say 'good hit!' or 'good shot!' or show by tightening their defense that they know you're about to smoke them. There's nothing like that feeling. But I feel that same way at home when my wife applauds me for bringing in a big business deal or brags to her friends about what a good father I am. It's that same feeling."

> "All those women in the men's magazines convey one message: 'I want you, and you are the most desirable man in the world.'"

During my clinical research for *The Lights of Tenth Street*, several experts told me that a chronic lack of affirmation is one reason so many men slip into pornography addiction. For whatever reason, they feel like less than a man, so they seek—and find!—affirmation in pornography. As one man pointed out, "All those women in the men's magazines convey one message: 'I want *you*, and you are the most desirable man in the world.' My wife may be nagging me at home, the kids may be disobedient, and I may be worried about messing up at work, but looking at the woman in that picture makes me feel like a *man*."

If affirmation is indeed everything, why should a man

have to look for it in other places when he has a wife who loves and respects him? There's nothing wrong with work, sports, or hobbies—it's wonderful for him to feel alive and encouraged in those pursuits—but they shouldn't have to be a retreat from an *un*affirming home life.

Create a safety zone

Obviously, if many of our men spend their workdays feeling like they are always being watched and judged, it is no wonder that they want to come home to a totally accepting environment, where they can safely let their guard down. Men need a place where they can make their mistakes in peace and not constantly worry that they are one misstep away from being exposed.

If we don't realize this and are perhaps too attentive to their mistakes at home, we risk creating a situation that is the opposite of what we want. Most of us *want* our men to be able to relax and truly open up to us. But in many ways, it is up to us to create the intimate, safe environment that makes that possible.

We may think that the adage "his home must be his haven" is antiquated and unnecessary these days, but that is far from the truth. In fact, as the workplace has gotten harsher and less loyal, more demanding and less tolerant of mistakes, I'd say it's even *more* important that a man's home be a haven. Most of the men I talked with *crave* a retreat from the daily pressure of always having to perform.

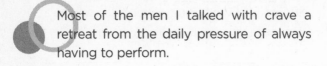

Most of the men I talked with crave a retreat from the daily pressure of always having to perform.

Supportive sex

Okay, girls, don't keel over from surprise when I tell you that this particular type of affirmation came up again and again. We'll talk more about how men view sex in a separate chapter, but I owe it to the many husbands who commented on its importance to at least mention it here.

"Sex plays a *huuuuuge* role in a man's self-confidence!" reported one husband via e-mail. "A man can be having a horrible time at work, rejection in his industry, and every other area can be going rotten—but if his wife wants him physically and affirms him in bed, he can handle the rest of the world no problem. Conversely, if he gets the same impostor message at home ('You don't measure up. Don't touch me'), it will devastate him far worse than any career blow."

Another man said, "The role of sex cannot be overstated. A great sex life will overshadow and overcome a multitude of impostor messages from the world."

THE GIFT OF CONFIDENCE

I heard from many men, "Men put a lot of pressure on themselves." On the survey, one husband pleaded, "I want my wife to know and understand my weaknesses, failings, shortcomings, and still want me. I need her to be my number one source of encouragement to become the man God created me to be."

We might think we wouldn't have the ability to change our man's feelings of workplace inadequacy, but we would be wrong. By staunchly supporting our men, showing that we believe in them, and providing an emotionally safe environment to come home to, we can help give them at least the emotional confidence they need to dive back into the daily workplace fray.

In his autobiography, *Jack: Straight from the Gut*, Jack Welch, the famous chairman and CEO of General Electric, provides an insight for businessmen that is important for every wife—and mother—to hear. Speaking about his mother, he wrote:

> Perhaps the greatest single gift she gave me was self-confidence. It's what I've looked for and tried to build in every executive who has ever worked with me. Confidence gives you courage and extends your

reach. It lets you take greater risks and achieve far more than you ever thought possible. Building self-confidence in others is a huge part of leadership. It comes from providing opportunities and challenges for people to do things they never imagined they could do—rewarding them after each success in every way possible.

> It's about sending the man we love into the world every day, alive with the belief that he can slay dragons.

A wife can give her husband that confidence (just as, hopefully, a husband can for his wife). It's not about being the supportive "little woman." It's about realizing that despite their veneer of confidence, our husbands really do "carry their treasures in fragile containers," and they crave our affirmation for how they did on that play. It's about sending the man we love into the world every day, alive with the belief that he can slay dragons.

Chapter 4

THE LONELIEST BURDEN

How His Need to Provide Weighs Your Man Down, and Why He Likes It That Way

Even if you made enough income to support your family's lifestyle, it would make no difference to the mental burden your husband feels to provide.

In my interviews I was startled to hear the explicit mental certainty most men had about their role as the family provider. Whatever a man's wife felt about it, whatever she did or didn't earn, he felt that providing was *his job*. Period.

I was surprised that so many men echoed the same conviction: "I love my wife, but I can't depend on her to provide. That's my job."

"I love my wife, but I can't depend on her to provide. That's my job."

In several interviews, the man's wife was sitting right next to him. One wife, shocked, turned to her husband and said, "But I've always worked! I've always contributed to the family budget!"

His gentle response: "You working or not is irrelevant. Not to the family budget—it does ease some of the financial pressure. But it is irrelevant to my *need* to provide."

"IT'S MY JOB..."

We have all heard that men want to be providers. They want to club the buffalo over the head and drag it back to the cave to their woman. But what few women understand is that this is not just an issue of "wanting to." Rather, it is a burden that presses heavily on them and won't let up.

Consider the stunning results from the survey. First, his need to provide goes so deep that even if you personally brought home enough money to nicely support the whole family, your man would probably *still* feel compelled to provide.

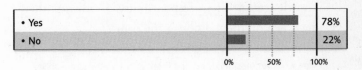

Suppose your wife/significant other earned enough to support your family's lifestyle. Would you still feel a compulsion to provide for your family? [Choose One Answer]

• Yes	78%
• No	22%

0%   50%   100%

It didn't matter whether the men were married or single, religious or not, old or young—three out of four felt this compulsion. The only major difference was an ethnic one: The compulsion was *stronger* among minority groups.

Does the big picture here surprise you as much as it did me? Popular culture often portrays men as willing freeloaders. What they really want to do, we're told, is park on the recliner and command the remote. But in reality, <u>for most men the drive to provide is so deeply rooted that almost nothing can relieve their feeling of duty.</u> It appears to be nothing less than an obsession—similar in some ways to women's obsessive body insecurity ("I wish I could lose weight!").

> For most men, the drive to provide is so deeply rooted that almost nothing can relieve their feeling of duty.

"And it's my job *all the time!*"

The second thing the survey revealed is that men not only carry this burden, but that it is *constant*. There's no respite— the <u>knowledge of their responsibility</u> is always there, <u>pressing down on them</u>. Look at the data:

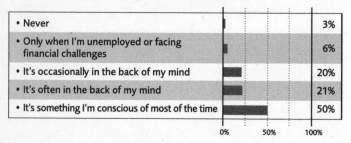

Under what circumstances do you think about your responsibility to provide for your family? [Choose One Answer]

• Never	3%
• Only when I'm unemployed or facing financial challenges	6%
• It's occasionally in the back of my mind	20%
• It's often in the back of my mind	21%
• It's something I'm conscious of most of the time	50%

Stop for a second and read those results slowly, until they sink in. A large majority of men (71 percent) say that their responsibility to provide is *always or often* on their mind. Think about what it must feel like to be conscious of this burden "most of the time"!

An employee at my local Costco described the provider impulse this way: "It's always in the back of my mind that I need to provide. A man won't feel like a man if he doesn't."

"Is it ever *not* in the back of your mind?" I asked.

"Nope," he declared. "If you're going to be the man, that's just the way it is."

THE INNER LIFE OF A PROVIDER

What drives this compulsion to provide? And since this need appears to be unchanging—despite our modern dual-income culture in which a wife can often provide for herself, thank you very much—what must we learn to recognize and (for the most part) accept about the way our men are wired?

Providing is at the core of a man's identity

Being a provider appears to be at the core of a man's identity as a male and as a person of worth: To be a man, he feels, means to be a provider. Even single men feel this way. On one long plane trip, I asked the unmarried man sitting next to me whether he felt a burden to provide even though he had no one to provide for. "It's still the same," he said. "You want to be in control of your life." He explained that if he didn't provide for himself, other people would have to, and he would no longer be in control.

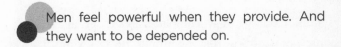

Men feel powerful when they provide. And they want to be depended on.

In other words, being the provider isn't just a burden, but a highly desirable goal. Men feel powerful when they provide. And they *want* to be depended on. The ability to take <u>care of those they feel responsible for</u> lies at the very center <u>of their sense of</u> personal significance.

I was telling one man how surprised I was at how *intense* guys are about being the provider. "Maybe you should see this as the flip side of how we think about sex," he offered. "About sex, men are pretty utilitarian and women are emotional. About money, work, or providing, women are utilitarian but men get emotional!"

Providing is a primary way to say "I love you"

For a man, bringing home a paycheck is love talk, pure and simple. He has something to prove ("I can take care of you, I am worthy of you") and he wants to deliver.

Even more pointedly, in a man's mind, providing for his wife is a central way of expressing his love. As one young man told me, "<u>My job is to worry about providing</u> so that my <u>wife doesn't have to. That's one way I show her I love her.</u>"

Long hours = love?

It's ironic that we may complain about our man's work habits, not realizing that he thinks he is saying "I love you"—*and we are complaining about it!* This dynamic is both confusing and distressing for men.

A conversation was relayed to me recently that highlights this irony. A couple we know had recently read *The*

Lights of Tenth Street, in which the main male character frequently travels, and his wife sadly wonders whether he cares more about work than her.

After reading this scene, our male friend—who also travels a lot—turned to his wife and asked, "Do *you* ever wonder that?"

Surprised, she answered, "Well, of course!"

"Why do you think I do work this much? It's because I care about you!"

Flabbergasted, he said, "Why do you think I *do* work this much? It's because I care about you!" He had been traveling for almost twenty-five years, and his wife had never understood that he viewed it as a sacrifice he made out of love and a desire to provide for her.

Providing accompanies his need to succeed

Now let's be honest—other motivations are also at work here. Many of the men I interviewed combined a selfless desire to provide with a powerful internal drive to succeed and find pleasure in their work. Half of the men surveyed agreed that if they worked a lot it was because they felt: "I've got to work a lot to get ahead, and I want to get ahead," or "I want to be working this much because I enjoy work," or both.

On the survey, one man echoed the feeling of many men I interviewed. He said the one thing he wished his wife knew was "that I enjoy my career and that being successful is important for me and for us."

Just as women can have multiple reasons for doing the things we value—including work—men do too. We should appreciate our mate's drive to work, provide, and succeed as long as there is some balance and the home relationship remains strong. In particular, we should be grateful if our mate is in the enviable position of loving what he does for a living.

Providing carries an ongoing risk of failure

Now let's make the connection between the provider impulse and the subject of the last chapter—your man's deep insecurity that he may not "cut it." It turns out that providing is *the* key arena where men experience the ongoing risk of failure.

> Providing is the key arena where men experience the ongoing risk of failure.

Paul of Tarsus said that the man who doesn't provide for his family is "worse than an infidel." As a woman I always assumed that was a command: "Provide for your family or you are worse than an infidel."

What I didn't realize was that, although it may in fact be a command, it is also a description of how terrible men feel about themselves when times are tight and they are not doing a good job of providing. Most men, as you now see, don't *need* that command. They are driven to provide no matter what. That statement could just as easily be read as an accurate reflection of internal angst—the horrible feeling that one is truly "worse than an infidel."

"I feel like my skin is being flayed off"

Because of this dynamic, men constantly worry about failure at work, layoffs, or a downturn in business. Since a majority of men (61 percent) said they regularly felt unappreciated at work, it appears that many truly think they are at risk. But because we see our men as talented and effective, we may not understand this fear and therefore may not realize how *strongly* they feel about doing whatever is necessary to protect their jobs and provide for their families.

If the worst happens and the family encounters financial problems, the man feels like a failure. Even if the financial problems have *nothing to do with him* (say, for example, his biggest client went out of business), if the end result is that you have to adjust your lifestyle, can't buy the children the birthday presents they asked for, or have trouble paying the mortgage, the man suffers emotional torture.

One man, whose business is currently in a very difficult season, described it this way: "Every day, with every step I take, I feel like my skin is being flayed off."

Providers can feel trapped

Every day, providers can feel a strange tension between wanting to be depended on and feeling trapped by that responsibility. The vast majority of men who put in long hours do so not just because they want to get ahead, but because they believe, as several men told me, "there is no other option." And they get frustrated when we don't understand that—particularly when they feel *we* are the source of some of the pressure.

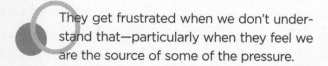

They get frustrated when we don't understand that—particularly when they feel we are the source of some of the pressure.

One very direct survey response made me wince—partly because I heard this same plea from a number of men I interviewed. This man wished he could tell his wife, "I feel confused. You want me home more (I travel each week and really wish I could be home), yet you want a new house, nice things, substantial income, etc. Please understand the catch-22 I am in. Due to past cutbacks with previous employers, I had to take this job. I feel like I am pushing two big rocks uphill."

Even when we're not pressuring our men materially, we can inadvertently pressure them in other ways, such as by complaining about long hours. For example, many of us secretly suspect that if our men would just tell their bosses no once in a while, they would be able to spend more time with us. Or we may worry that our men just don't want to be with us very much. So on the survey I just *had* to test these suspicions. You know how many men were actually thinking one of those two things? Just a tiny fraction!

Instead, the vast majority of the men surveyed (82 percent) had what I would characterize as an unselfish motivation, answering that if they didn't work that hard, they would let their family and/or the organization down. Most of these men answered, "If I don't work this hard, I feel like my job might be at risk, and I do have to provide for my family," or "There is no way to support our family lifestyle without working this hard—I guess I could find a job with fewer hours, but it wouldn't pay enough." Furthermore, half of those men went out of their way to add that they didn't *want* to be away from their families so much!

Consider the response of one surveyed man, whose mate had probably challenged him about his priorities: "My priorities ARE my family. I wish I knew of some way not to work so much, or to be available more, but I don't know how to make this work otherwise. I wish she was more aware of this."

Don't get me wrong—I am the last person to advise sitting in silence if you're concerned about your man's time away from family. I tend to go too far the other direction—as my husband can attest! But if you can put yourself in your husband's shoes and understand how he might feel trapped, he's more likely to see your concern as supportive rather than antagonistic.

Providing means earning enough for both present and future

For men, the need to provide for today is amplified by anxieties about also providing for the future. Essentially, they feel like they have to earn *two* incomes—one to get the family through the present and the other to see the family through the long retirement years. One man wrote, "I wish my wife would understand that I am not only providing for the present, but I am trying to save for our golden years."

Many working men mentioned anxiety because they had

seen retired men lose their emotional rudder once this huge part of their identity disappeared. They said that when a man gets a social security or pension check without feeling like he is earning it, he feels like he has "lost his purpose."

This dynamic may partly explain why men who are unemployed or on welfare so often get depressed and lose their motivation. They feel like they have failed at being a provider, have lost their purpose, and are less than a man.

SO HOW DO WE RESPOND?

Now that we grasp how overwhelming the provider impulse is, what should we do about it?

Reconsider existing areas of conflict

Ladies, we must face the fact that our mate feels caught, with few options, on provider issues. And he probably also feels deeply misunderstood by us. Take a look at where both facts may have impacted your relationship.

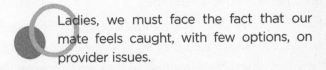

Ladies, we must face the fact that our mate feels caught, with few options, on provider issues.

For example, once I understood Jeff's provider burden, I suddenly grasped that an unwillingness to "stand up to" his boss wasn't some uncharacteristic weakness, but a strong desire to continue to be able to pay the mortgage! (Which meant that my primary response shouldn't be criticism, but appreciation.) Some women might suddenly realize the pressure they have inadvertently been putting on their husbands by coming home with new shopping bags every day—while others may grasp just how painful it is for their husbands to earn less than they do. Others may understand—as one representative man wrote—"the stress of feeling that you are asking him to choose between one huge need (to provide financial security for you) and another (to show you he really does care about family time)."

Of course, just because we *understand* a man's assumptions on these issues doesn't mean that we will always *agree* with them! For example, we may be very willing to accept a tighter budget in return for a more family-friendly job. But regardless, understanding where our man is coming from is essential to any kind of productive conversation.

Help relieve the pressure

Many of us have faced difficult financial seasons in recent years, and obviously that's hard for us women too. It is easy to get nervous and blame our husband or pressure him to "do something." But most men don't need more pressure. They've got that in spades internally.

Instead, they need our steadfast belief that they will solve this problem and our steadfast offer to help them do what it takes to stay afloat. That may mean showing our willingness to bring in more income ourselves or expressing excitement about staying with friends at the beach in the off-season instead of going on that romantic Caribbean vacation. (I say *excitement* rather than *willingness* because a man will internalize your disappointment as a personal failure to provide.)

> A man will internalize your disappointment as a personal failure to provide.

Several men have told me that, most of all, the best thing their mate can do is to show that she *realizes* how tight things are by refusing to spend money unnecessarily. That, combined with our emotional support, does wonders for the man's feeling that "we can get through this."

But how can we be emotionally supportive when *we* need support? Having gone through a difficult financial season with my husband, I can say that the answer is to cast our cares for provision on the Lord rather than on our men. In the end, it is His job to carry the burden. In the awe-inspiring conclusion to the *Lord of the Rings* trilogy, when the hero is completely exhausted from carrying his terrible burden, his best friend lifts him to his shoulders, crying, "I can't carry it for you—but I can carry you!" By praying for our husbands and looking to the Lord rather than to our circumstances, we trust Him to carry both our husband and his burden. Then from the overflow of our hearts, we can give back to and encourage our men.

Encourage and appreciate him

One man gave a great summation of what a man needs most, whether a couple is "in plenty or in want." "Thank him regularly for providing. He forgets quickly."

Most of us want to support our men, and in this case being a support means understanding them, appreciating them, and helping to relieve the pressure they feel rather than adding to it.

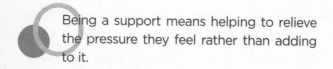

Being a support means helping to relieve the pressure they feel rather than adding to it.

One husband put it this way: "Make sure he knows your pleasure in any financial progress so he knows all his obsessive hard work was worth it. And when he comes in really late from an extra long day at the office, surprise him with a thank-you gift. Use your imagination."

Chapter 5

SEX CHANGES EVERYTHING

Why Sex Unlocks a Man's Emotions (Guess Who Holds the Key?)

Your sexual desire for your husband profoundly affects his sense of well-being and confidence in all areas of his life.

It's not exactly a shocker to say that men want more sex. We've known that—and giggled about it with our girlfriends—since junior high. But do you know how strongly your man feels this need and—more to the point—*why?*

On each survey and in my random interviews around the country, an urgent theme emerged: Men want more sex than they are getting. And what's more, they believe that the women who love them *don't seem to realize that this is a crisis*—not only for the man, but for the relationship.

Why on earth is it a *crisis*? After all, a lot of other legitimate needs get in the way. Like sleep. Isn't sex just a primal, biological urge that he really should be able to do without? Well…no. For your husband, sex is more than just a physical need. Lack of sex is as emotionally serious to him as, say, his sudden silence would be to you, were he simply to stop communicating with you. It is just as wounding to him, just as much a legitimate grievance—and just as dangerous to your marriage.

Since this book is only about things we tend to miss or misunderstand about our men, I'll skip the usual data on the *power* of your man's sexual needs and focus instead on their *importance* to him as a person. In other words—not on the physical need, but on the overwhelming emotional need for sex that you may not even know he has.

SEX FILLS A POWERFUL *EMOTIONAL* NEED

Although popular opinion portrays males as one giant sex gland with no emotions attached, that is the furthest thing from the truth. But because men don't tend to describe their sexual needs in emotional terms, we women may not realize that.

In a very deep way, your man often feels isolated and burdened by secret feelings of inadequacy. Making love with you assures him that you find him desirable, salves a deep sense of loneliness, and gives him the strength and well-being necessary to face the world with confidence. And, of course, sex also makes him feel loved—in fact, he can't feel completely loved without it.

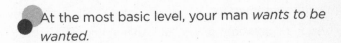

At the most basic level, your man *wants to be wanted.*

At the most basic level, your man *wants to be wanted.* Look at the overwhelming response from the second professional survey. (The first survey did not cover this subject.)

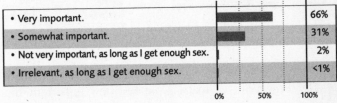

With regard to sex, for some men it is sufficient to be sexually gratified whenever they want. For other men it is also important to feel wanted and desired by their wife. How important is it to you to also feel sexually wanted and desired by your wife? [Choose One Answer]

• Very important.	66%
• Somewhat important.	31%
• Not very important, as long as I get enough sex.	2%
• Irrelevant, as long as I get enough sex.	<1%

This topic earned the highest degree of unanimity of any question: 97 percent of men said "getting enough sex" wasn't, by itself, enough—they wanted to feel wanted.

One man I interviewed summed it up like this: "Everyone thinks women are more emotional than men. And everyone thinks that when it comes to sex, guys just want to 'do it,' and women are more into the emotion and cuddling of it. So women think there are no emotions there. But there *are*, and when you say no, you are messing with all those emotions."

And it's not only a flat "no" that hurts. The survey showed that *even if they were getting all the sex they wanted,* three out of four men would still feel empty if their wife wasn't both engaged and satisfied.

Imagine that your wife offers all the sex that you want, but does it reluctantly or simply to accommodate your sexual needs. Will you be sexually satisfied? [Choose One Answer]

• Yes	26%
• No	74%

0%   50%   100%

As one survey taker explained, "I think that my wife after twenty-some years of marriage knows how important my need for sex is, but I wish she knew how important it is to me that she *needs* me sexually. She probably does not need sex so much, but I need her to want and need sex with me."

Reality check!

I believe that most of us aren't manipulatively withholding something we know is critical to our husband's sense of well-being. Much more likely is that after a long day at the office or with the kids, we just don't feel an overwhelming desire to rip off our husband's clothes and go at it. I suspect we simply don't realize the emotional consequences of our response (or lack of one) and view his desire for sex more as a physical desire or even an insensitive demand. Once we truly comprehend the truth behind our husband's advances, we're more likely to *want* to respond.

> We may not realize the emotional consequences of our response—or lack of one.

WHY IS SEX SO IMPORTANT?

What kinds of emotional needs does your sexual interest meet for your man? In the written survey comments and in my interviews, I noticed two parallel trends—the great benefits a fulfilling sex life creates in a man's inner life and, conversely, the wounds created when lovemaking is reluctant or lacking.

Benefit #1: Fulfilling sex makes him feel loved and desired.

Not surprisingly, the first thing that surfaced from the survey comments was that having a *regular*, mutually enjoyed sex life was critical to the man's feeling of being loved and desired. One eloquent plea captured it perfectly:

> I wish that my wife understood that making a priority of meeting my intimacy needs is the loudest and clearest way she can say, "You are more important to me than anything else in the world." It is a form of communication that speaks more forcefully, with less room for misinterpretation, than any other.

The reason *why* this message is needed is that many men—even those with close friendships—seem to live with a deep sense of loneliness that is quite foreign to us oh-so-relational women. And making love is the purest salve for that loneliness.

One man told me, "I feel like I go out into the ring every day and fight the fight. It's very lonely. That's why, when the bell rings, I want my wife to be there for me."

Another related that sentiment to the power of fulfilling sex. "A man really does feel isolated, even with his wife. But in making love, there is one other person in this world that you can be completely vulnerable with and be totally accepted and nonjudged. It is a solace that goes very deep into the heart of a man."

"Making love is a solace that goes very deep into the heart of a man."

This is one reason why some men may make advances at times that seem the *furthest* from sexual. One woman relayed a story about her husband wanting to make love after a funeral for a close relative. Making love was a comfort and a way of being wrapped in her love.

Benefit #2: Fulfilling sex gives him confidence.

Your desire for him goes beyond making him feel wanted and loved. As we touched on in the "Impostor" chapter, your desire is a bedrock form of support that gives him power to face the rest of his daily life with a sense of confidence and well-being.

By now most of us have seen the television commercials for Viagra in which a man's colleagues and friends repeatedly stop him and ask what's "different" about him. New haircut? Been working out? Promotion? Nope, the man tells them all, with a little smile.

One man I interviewed brought up those ads. "Every man immediately understands what that commercial is saying—it's all about guys feeling good about themselves. The ad portrays a truth that all men intuitively recognize. They are more confident and alive when their sex life is working."

On the survey, again, three out of four men agreed.

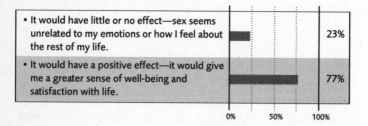

Imagine that your wife was an interested and motivated sexual partner, and you therefore had an active love life. How would having sex with her as often as you wanted affect your emotional state? [Choose One Answer]

• It would have little or no effect—sex seems unrelated to my emotions or how I feel about the rest of my life.	23%
• It would have a positive effect—it would give me a greater sense of well-being and satisfaction with life.	77%

Once my eyes were opened to this truth, I realized how often I'd heard the "man code" for this fact, but failed to understand it. When men had told me they "felt better" when they got more sex, I had just assumed they meant physically better.

But as one husband told me, "What happens in the bedroom really does affect how I feel the next day at the office."

Another wrote, "Sex is a release of day-to-day pressures...and *seems to make everything else better*" (emphasis mine).

Once we see how central a man's sex life is to his emotional well-being, we need to know what happens in his heart when he doesn't get what he's looking for.

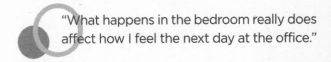

"What happens in the bedroom really does affect how I feel the next day at the office."

Wound #1: "If she doesn't want to, I feel incredible rejection."

As much as men want sex, most of them would rather go out and clip the hedges in the freezing rain than make love with a wife who appears to be responding out of duty. My husband, Jeff, explained: "The guy isn't going to be rejected by the hedges. And that's the issue. If she's just responding because she has to, he's being rejected by his wife."

Again, keeping in mind that what he wants most is for you to desire him, try to see this rejection issue from the man's point of view. If we agree, but don't make an effort to get really engaged with the man we love, he hears us saying, "You're incapable of turning me on even when you try, and I really don't care about what matters deeply to you." On the other hand, if we don't agree at all, but throw out the classic "Not tonight, dear," he hears, "You're so undesirable that you can't compete with a pillow...and I really don't care about what matters deeply to you."

Although we might just be saying we don't want sex *at that point in time,* he hears the much more painful message that we don't want *him.*

Here's what the men themselves said on the survey:

- "She doesn't understand that I feel loved by sexual caressing, and if she doesn't want to, I feel incredible rejection."

- "When she says no, I feel that I am REJECTED. 'No' is *not* no to sex—as she might feel. It is no to me as I am. And I am vulnerable as I ask or initiate. It's plain and simple rejection."

- "She doesn't understand how even her occasional dismissals make me feel less desirable. I can't resist her. I wish that I, too, were irresistible. She says I am. But her ability to say no so easily makes it hard to believe."

"'No' is not no to sex—as she might feel. It is no to me as I am."

This feeling of personal rejection, and a sense that his wife doesn't really desire him, tends to lead a man into darker waters.

Wound #2: Your lack of desire can send him into depression.

If your sexual desire gives your husband a sense of well-being and confidence, you can understand why an ongoing perception that you don't desire him would translate into a nagging lack of confidence, withdrawal, and depression.

The men I talked to scoffed at my tentative suggestion that a string of similar rejections wouldn't necessarily mean that their wives were rejecting them as men. They warned that any woman sending those signals would undermine the loving environment she wants most because, as one man said, "She is going to have one depressed man on her hands."

A man can't just turn off the physical and emotional importance of sex, which is why its lack can be compared to the emotional pain you'd feel if your husband simply stopped talking to you. Consider the painful words of this truly deprived husband—words that other men, upon reading them, call "heartbreaking":

We've been married for a long time. I deeply regret and resent the lack of intimacy of nearly any kind for the duration of our marriage. I feel rejected, ineligible, insignificant, lonely, isolated, and abandoned as a result. Not having the inter-action I anticipated prior to marriage is like a treasure lost and irretrievable. It causes deep resentment and hurt within me. This in turn fosters anger and feelings of alienation.

HOW CAN WE OVERCOME THE "SEX GAP"?

I can't tell you how often I heard a man's not-at-all-veiled appeal for his wife to not only desire him, but to *do something* about it. Although every intimate relationship has its own story, here are a few ways to begin:

Choose to love him in the way he needs

Okay, if you're like me, you've probably been viewing his sexual need as mostly physical—*important*, yes, but probably also *optional*. By comparison, when you've been tugged on by little hands all day, your need for sleep can seem both impor-tant *and* immediately necessary. And, yes, if you view sex as a purely physical need, it might indeed seem comparable to sleep. But once you realize that your man is actually saying, "This is essential to my feeling of being loved and desired by you, and is critical to counteract my stress, my fears, and my loneliness," well…that suddenly puts it in a different category. So how might you respond?

> Know that you're responding to a tender heart hiding behind all that testosterone.

First, know that you're responding to a tender heart hiding behind all that testosterone. If at all possible, respond to his advances with your full emotional involvement, knowing that you're touching his *heart*. But if responding physically seems out of the question, let your words be *heart* words—reassuring, affirming, adoring. Do everything in your power—*using words and actions your husband understands*—to keep those pangs of personal rejection from striking the man you love. Leave him in no doubt that you love to love him.

And remember, if you do respond physically but do it just to "meet his needs" without getting engaged, you're not actually meeting his needs. In fact, you might as well send him out to clip the hedges. So enjoy God's intimate gift, and make the most of it!

Get involved…and have more fun, too

One man on the churchgoer's survey was particularly blunt. "The woman needs to play an active role in the sex life. She needs to tell her mate what she needs, wants, and feels. Passive wife = boring life."

Whew!

I discovered that many men love the secret knowledge of having a wife who is sexually motivated. A few years ago, I overheard a thirty-year-old single friend telling Jeff what he wanted in a wife. "I want a wife who is a model of Christian virtue—godly, faithful, and always kind to others." A grin crept into his voice. "But when I get her home…!"

"It's like that song 'Behind Closed Doors' from the seventies," a married friend told me recently. "That's what every man wants—the girl next door in the living room and a wildcat in the bedroom."

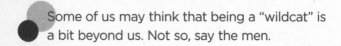

Some of us may think that being a "wildcat" is a bit beyond us. Not so, say the men.

Now, some of us may laugh at that and think that being a "wildcat" is a bit beyond us. Not so, say the men. All that means, they say, is a wife who makes the first move once in a while and who brings all of her attentions and passion for her man to bed with her. Do that, and watch your husband light up with delight!

If you need help, get it

I recognize that some women might very much wish that they *could* respond more wholeheartedly to their husbands' sexual needs, but feel stopped in their tracks for various personal reasons. I don't want to add any more frustration. I do, however, want to encourage you to get the personal or professional help you need to move forward. The choice to pursue healing will be worth it, both for you and the man you love.

Make sex a priority

An excerpt from a *Today's Christian Woman* article captures this issue—and provides an important challenge to change our thinking. The author starts by admitting that although her husband really wanted to make love more often, it "just wasn't one of my priorities." She then describes a subsequent revelation:

> I felt what I did all day was meet other people's needs. Whether it was caring for my children, working in ministry, or washing my husband's clothes, by the end of the day I wanted to be done need-meeting. I wanted my pillow and a magazine. But God prompted me: *Are the "needs" you meet for your husband the needs he wants met?*

If our daughters weren't perfectly primped, he didn't complain. If the kitchen floor needed mopping, he didn't say a word. And if he didn't have any socks to wear, he simply threw them in the washer himself.

I soon realized I regularly said "no" to the one thing he asked of me. I sure wasn't making myself available to my husband by militantly adhering to my plan for the day.... Would the world end if I didn't get my tires rotated? I'd been so focused on what I wanted to get done and what my children needed, I'd cut my hubby out of the picture.

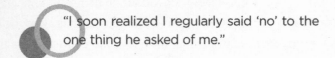

"I soon realized I regularly said 'no' to the one thing he asked of me."

Are the many other things that take our time and energy truly as important as this one? Now would be a good time to reevaluate priorities with the help of our husbands so they know that we are taking this seriously.

Getting those "love signals" right

In closing, I thought it would be encouraging to look in on how one average husband and wife handled this issue. Mark and Anne had a good marriage in general. They had been married fifteen years when Mark noticed their sex life starting to wane. Anne was not responding the way she used to, was just not as interested, too busy, too tired. They didn't stop making love, but as Mark says, "It just seemed to be less of a priority for her."

Mark is a businessman, and he sometimes works long hours, which used to be a source of grief for Anne. Years earlier she had sat down with him and explained that it wasn't so much the hours that hurt her, but that he didn't come home when he said he would. She told him that he was a great husband, but that this one thing made her feel very uncared-for. She told him that his willingness to tell her a realistic time when he'd be home and stick to it was— for her—one of the most important signals of his love. Mark understood and that became a top priority for him.

Now, years later, Mark sat down with Anne and told her that he was concerned about the drop-off in their sex life. He drew a parallel to Anne's need for him to be home when promised. He said, "I could be a great husband but not do this one thing that is really important to you, and I'd still fail at making you feel loved. Having sex like we used to, having you be responsive to me, is the same thing for me."

Anne had never understood it that way, and it was

important for her to hear that she could be a great wife, but if she didn't respond to her husband's sexual desires—one of his most important "love signals"—she'd still fail at making him feel loved. As Mark now says, "It clicked for her. And that changed everything."

Has your husband been sending you signals?

Has your husband been sending you signals that he is unhappy about your responsiveness to him? It's possible that he may wish he could explain this to you, but doesn't know how. Or maybe he's tried, but you've discounted the importance of his request.

Having heard from so many men on this, I would urge you: Don't discount it. It is more important to him—and to your relationship and therefore your own joy in marriage—than you can imagine.

Now that you understand the tender places in your husband's heart, hopefully you have developed compassion for him and the way he is wired. Let's take that compassion and understanding with us as we examine the next area of his inner life.

Chapter 6

KEEPER OF THE VISUAL ROLODEX

Why It's So Natural for Him to Look and So Hard to Forget What He's Seen

Even happily married men struggle with being pulled toward live and recollected images of other women.

Scene One: Doug, a successful businessman with a wife and kids, has traveled to California for a business deal. The conference room fills with top executives, so each one can give him a presentation. The first executive, a very attractive woman, walks to the whiteboard. She has a great figure, Doug notices, and her well-fitted suit shows it off tastefully. As she begins her presentation, the woman is friendly but all business.

Scene Two: I'm talking to a series of randomly selected Christian men who are serious about their faith and (if they're married) genuinely devoted to their wives. I describe Scene One above and tell them it is straight out of my novel *The Lights of Tenth Street.* Then I ask each man a question: "If you were Doug, what would be going through your mind as the female executive makes her presentation?"

Here are some of their answers:

- *"Great body… Stop it! What am I thinking?"*
- "I check to see if she's wearing a wedding ring."
- "I wonder if she finds me attractive."
- "I feel an instant tightening in my gut."
- *"I bet she's using those curves to sell this deal."*
- *"Look at her face, look at her face, look at her face…"*
- "It is hard for me to concentrate on her presentation because I'm trying so hard to look at her face and not her body."
- "I have to be ruthless about pushing back these *images*—and they keep intruding."
- *"I wonder what's under that nice suit? Stop it. Concentrate on the presentation."*
- "About two minutes into her talk, I'd be remembering a scene from a porn video I saw when I was fifteen."

- "If I'm not careful, a few minutes later I might be wondering what she's like in bed."

If you had been with me, listening to those men, what would *you* be thinking? I confess that their answers both amazed and dismayed me. Yet as I heard men I trusted reveal similar reactions over and over, I realized that this must be *normal*.

Although I'd always heard that men are visual, I had never really understood what that actually *meant*. I had been totally oblivious.

WHAT "MEN ARE VISUAL" MEANS

Here's the insight I stumbled on by accident, which has radically reshaped my understanding of men:

> Even happily married men are instinctively pulled
> to visually "consume" attractive women, and these
> images can be just as alluring whether they are live
> or recollected.

Two areas of this "men are visual" thing surfaced that I, at least, didn't really get before:

- First, a woman with a great body is an "eye magnet" that is incredibly difficult to avoid, and even if a man forces himself not to look, he is acutely aware of her presence.

- Second, even when no such eye magnet is present, each man has a "mental Rolodex" of stored images that can intrude into his thoughts without warning or can be called up at will.

If you're among the 25 percent of women who describe themselves as "visual," this "revelation" may not seem surprising. But for the rest of us, it may seem a mystery—or worse. We might even experience it as a personal failure on our part (for not being enough of a woman to keep his attention) or as a personal betrayal on his (why would a loving and committed husband have to push back images of other women *at all*?).

Thankfully, as we delve deeper, discovering how hardwired this compulsion is—and how *little* it has to do with us—is oddly encouraging. Actually, it is *two* separate but related compulsions. Let's keep an open mind and look at them, together.

Compulsion #1: A man can't *not* want to look.

In the survey, we created a scene similar to Doug's and asked men to predict their responses. Consider the results:

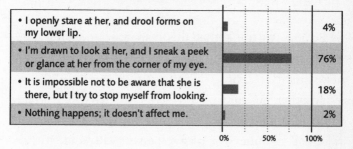

Imagine you are sitting alone in a train station and a woman with a great body walks in and stands in a nearby line. What is your reaction to the woman? [Choose One Answer]

• I openly stare at her, and drool forms on my lower lip.	4%
• I'm drawn to look at her, and I sneak a peek or glance at her from the corner of my eye.	76%
• It is impossible not to be aware that she is there, but I try to stop myself from looking.	18%
• Nothing happens; it doesn't affect me.	2%

0%   50%   100%

The first fact is that a whopping 98 percent of men put their response to an eye-catching woman in "can't *not* be attracted" categories (only 2 percent were unaffected by a woman with a great body). Interestingly, the results were essentially the same for men who described themselves as happily married believers.

Many men explained the power of this desire to look, even when they tried *not* to or when the attractive woman in question left their line of sight. One faithful husband whom I highly trust confessed, "If I see a woman with a great body walk into Home Depot and I close my eyes or turn away until she passes, for the next half hour I'm keenly aware that she's in there somewhere. I'm ashamed to say that, more than once, I've gone looking down the aisles, hoping to catch a glimpse."

"More than once, I've gone looking down the aisles, hoping to catch a glimpse."

I'd love to think that this man was an aberration—except that all the men I shared his quote with said, "That's *exactly* right!"

Another husband with a happy twenty-year marriage described another typical scenario: "My wife and I recently went out to dinner at a nice restaurant with some friends. The hostess was extremely attractive with a great figure and that spark that reaches out and grabs a man's attention. For the rest of the night, it was impossible not to be aware that she was across the restaurant, walking around. Our group had a great time with our lovely wives, but I guarantee you that our wives didn't know that every man at that table was acutely aware of that woman's presence and was doing his utmost not to look in that direction."

Now, think back to the opening of this book. These examples clarify why Jeff would suddenly turn his head as we walked the streets of New York: He was choosing to honor me. He had just seen an attractive woman and was forcing himself to look away so the image would not linger.

And that brings us to the second fact.

Compulsion #2: A man has a mental Rolodex of sensual images.

We've all heard that the male half of the population thinks about sex a lot. What I didn't realize was that they aren't exactly *thinking* about sex (as in, *I wonder if my wife will be in the mood tonight*). Rather, they're *picturing* it, or picturing a sexual image. And those pictures aren't necessarily of their wives. They are often images that have been involuntarily burned in their brains just by living in today's culture—images that can arise without warning.

You might be wondering, *What kinds of images?* Apparently just about anything: the memory of an intimate time with you (good) or the memory of a *Playboy* magazine (bad). It could be a recollection of the shapely woman who walked through the parking lot two minutes ago or an on-line porn site he saw two years ago. These images often arise without warning, even if the guy doesn't want them. Or specific images can be recalled on purpose. As several men put it, "I have an unending supply of images in my head, stretching back to my teens."

Images often arise without warning, even if the guy doesn't want them.

The survey results were clear:

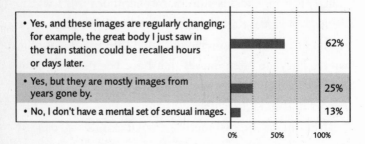

Many men have a mental set of sensual images that rise up or can be conjured up in their minds. Does this apply to you? [Choose One Answer]

• Yes, and these images are regularly changing; for example, the great body I just saw in the train station could be recalled hours or days later.	62%
• Yes, but they are mostly images from years gone by.	25%
• No, I don't have a mental set of sensual images.	13%

In total, 87 percent of men say these images pop up in their heads. When you break down the demographics, it is roughly the same across the board—whether men are old or young, happily married or single, religious or not.

The Tom Cruise conversation

One day, during the time I was trying to come to terms with these findings, Jeff and I were riding in the car, discussing what I was discovering. Jeff confessed that he didn't understand why I was so surprised. Here's how our conversation went from there:

> *Jeff:* "But you knew men are visual, right?"
>
> *Me:* "Well, yes, of course. But since most women

aren't, I just didn't get it. I just don't experience things the same way you do."

Jeff: "See, I'm not sure I really believe that."

Me: "Well, it's true!"

Jeff: "Maybe we just use different language to describe it. For example, think of a movie star that you find physically attractive—Tom Cruise, say. After we've seen one of his movies, how many times will that attractive image rise up in your mind the next day?"

Me: "Never."

Jeff: "I must not be explaining myself correctly. I mean, how many times will a thought of what he looked like with his shirt off just sort of pop up in your head?"

Me: "Never."

Jeff: "Never—as in *never?*"

Me: "Zero times. It just doesn't happen."

Jeff: (After a long pause) "Wow."

That was the end of that conversation, but it wasn't the end of the issue. When my husband recently told this story to our home group, he confessed that at first he thought I was embarrassed to admit that I really might have pictures of Tom Cruise in my head! It wasn't until he watched me tell the story to a group of women, and watched most of the woman say "never" right along with me, that the lightning bolt hit.

> "After we've seen one of his movies, how many times will that attractive image rise up in your mind the next day?"

Our little exchange did more to teach Jeff and me how each of us is wired—and *not* wired—than almost anything else. And I hope my new understanding is helping me be more supportive and protective of my husband in today's culture.

It's a minefield out there...

For those of us who aren't visual, it's hard to imagine that a man could have no control over something popping up in his head. We also may not recognize that in our sex-saturated culture, the very act of living is a minefield of possible triggers and potential images that could be recalled days or years later.

To use a common example, prime-time television commercials often flash sensual two-second images—say, of a woman undressing—that are up on the screen and gone before the man can look away. Nothing he can do. *Boom*, it's added to the mental Rolodex, whether he wants it or not.

Mental Rolodexes on speed-dial

When I asked men how often a sensual thought or image barged into their consciousness, many of them said something like "all the time." Of course, I wanted to know what "all the time" meant!

"If you're talking about a teenage boy, 'all the time' means *all the time*," one forty-year-old man explained. "It would be fairly unusual for a teenage guy to go a couple of hours without an involuntary image—and then when he does, he could spend half an hour straight on the subject. A twenty-something man also has a pretty difficult time. Once you reach your thirties and forties, you're a little more settled and those thoughts are more often triggered by something."

But once those thoughts are triggered, he and others clarified, an image could rise up two or three times a minute! And they also said that if the man is highly visually oriented, and if that temptation is entertained *at all*, it is even more difficult to get rid of.

THIS IS NORMAL?

Okay, let's take a deep breath for a second. For some of us, this is a lot to take in. For others, it's no big deal. Also, if you are "visual," you may more readily understand your husband's struggle. And don't worry—you're normal. But it's important for the rest of us to realize that our men are normal too. As the national survey showed, this temptation is common to every man. And as my interviewees emphasized, it has *no* bearing on their devotion to their wives.

Before we go any further, we should make a critical distinction: Temptations are *not* sins. (The Bible states that "Jesus was tempted in every way.") What we *do* with those temptations is the issue, and we'll get to that in a moment.

For now, let's sort out the progression of male responses to see which are involuntary and which most definitely are not.

> Temptations are *not* sins. What we *do* with those temptations is the issue.

Step 1: For every man, sensual images and thoughts arrive involuntarily.

Daniel Weiss, the media and sexuality analyst at Focus on the Family, told me, "I would emphasize to women that, yes, men do have these thoughts whether they want them or not."

In addition, the man's initial temptation is often not only unintentional, but automatic. If the stimulus is there (a great figure in a tight outfit), so is the response. As one man put it, "It doesn't even register that I thought *great body* until two seconds later!" A man cannot prevent those *initial* thoughts or images from intruding.

Don't believe me? Let me illustrate.

Don't read this.

No really, don't read it. Just look at the letters.

Impossible, isn't it? There is no way to just notice the letters without reading the word. That's what it's like for a guy. His brain reads "good body" without his even realizing it.

One man provided this analogy. "If you are nearsighted, everything is fuzzy without glasses. With your glasses, everything is in sharp focus. If a babe walks into Starbucks, other women sort of see fuzzy—all they see is that a woman is there. But all the men in the room suddenly have their 'glasses' on—that woman is in sharp focus, and it's really hard not to stare at her."

This distinction actually debunks the popular assumption that all the trouble starts because "men have roving eyes." A better understanding is that there are roving women—and men can't not notice their existence!

Step 2: Every man's involuntary physical impulse is to enjoy the feelings associated with these thoughts and images.

Because men are hardwired to be sexual hunters, every thought and image related to that pursuit comes associated with powerful feelings. When a sensual image enters a man's mind (or a great body enters his line of sight), it brings a rush of sexual pleasure—a short-term pleasure that, hopefully, the man denies himself in order to honor God, his wife, or his mental purity and thus establish deeper pleasure down the road.

> Hopefully, the man denies himself the short-term pleasure in order to honor his wife.

One married man told me, "It is pleasurable—in a small way—in the same way that sex is pleasurable. And forcing myself to remove that thought from my mind is sometimes as difficult as it would be to stop in the middle of sex."

Another wrote: "When an image plays on a man's brain or he gazes at an attractive woman, it's not just pure lust. There's a thrill there. And a man can go back to that adrenaline rush by entertaining those images."

In my clinical research for *The Lights of Tenth Street*, I heard over and over again how much men gravitate toward something that gives them an inner excitement, an illicit thrill—which helps us then understand why some men can get trapped by pornography.

Step 3: But every man can make a choice—to dwell on the images and thoughts, or to dismiss them.

This choice is the critical distinction between temptation and sin. Once an image intrudes in a man's head, he can either linger on it and possibly even start a mental parade, or tear it down immediately and "take every thought captive," as the Bible puts it.

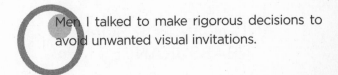

Men I talked to make rigorous decisions to avoid unwanted visual invitations.

Most of the men I talked to take this choice extremely seriously. They make rigorous decisions to avoid unwanted visual invitations, to turn away from those that arise, and—when unwanted pictures arise anyway—to rip them down with all sorts of diversionary tactics. I heard that mentally running through baseball scores and household projects were popular thought substitutes! Honestly, it sounds exhausting.

So although few men can stop an involuntary image from popping up in their heads, and few men can stop themselves from *wanting* to look, they can (and do) exercise the discipline to stop themselves from actually doing so. On the survey, the biggest factor in whether a man made this choice wasn't whether he was older, married, or happy in his relationship (all of those mattered, but in small numbers). It was whether he regularly attended religious services. Confirming this, nearly *half* of the men on the follow-up churchgoers survey said they would try to stop themselves from looking.

It is vital that we understand just how much strength and discipline that choice requires so that we can appreciate what our men try to do for us every day in this minefield of a culture.

AND NOW FOR SOME REASSURANCES

It's also vital to recognize that, after all these generalizations, there are several critical reassuring elements which are just as much a part of a man's inner life.

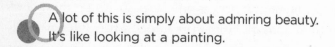

A lot of this is simply about admiring beauty. It's like looking at a painting.

Reassurance #1: His temptation is often not primarily sexual.

One distinction I heard repeatedly from men was that "wanting to look" often wasn't primarily sexual. Instinctive? Yes. Physical? Sure. But not necessarily sexual.

One man told me, "What you may not realize is that a lot

of this is simply about admiring beauty. It is pleasurable to look at that good-looking woman. It's like looking at a painting. You're not just thinking, *Let's go to a motel and shack up.* Women don't necessarily look at a man and admire him as a thing of beauty, but men will do that. It's like walking through an art gallery. A man may look, despite himself. But it's not necessarily a sexual thing."

Reassurance #2: Every man is different.

Also, because every man is different, every man experiences a different level of visual temptation. For some men, an involuntary sensual image may be little more than a nuisance, while others might find it a real stumbling block.

Here's a comparison that some of us might recognize all too well. At a dessert party, I might struggle for two hours with the fact that a chocolate mousse cake is across the room, calling my name. But the person standing next to me might be able to put that temptation out of her mind. (Don't you just hate those people?!)

Since everyone is different, we shouldn't jump to conclusions or pass blanket judgments.

Reassurance #3: It's not because of you.

Upon learning all of this, some of us may secretly wonder, *What's wrong with me? Am I not attractive enough?* We suspect that our husband's struggle arises because of our own flaws, not just because he's a man.

But hearing this from every man I interviewed made clear that this truly is—as the title of a popular book puts it—*Every Man's Battle*.

In the biblical book of Job, the title character makes a telling statement: "I made a covenant with my eyes not to look with lust upon a young woman."

Why would Job need to take such a step? God describes him as "the finest man in all the earth—a man of complete integrity" (Job 1:8). Surely, the "finest man in all the earth" wouldn't even *have* this struggle!

But Job was a man. You love your husband as a man, and this is part of what makes him a man. Even if you were a bikini model, your husband would still have this vulnerability.

Furthermore, many men echoed this husband's sentiment: "You have to realize: If men could, most would shut off their temptation to look at other women in a second. We loathe this temptation as much as our wives do!"

> Why would Job need to take such a step? God describes him as "the finest man in all the earth."

Reassurance #4: This doesn't impact his feelings for you!

Finally, and most important, we must grasp this fact: A man's human temptation has, as one man put it, "no impact whatsoever on my feelings for my wife."

A man married more than twenty-five years explained:

> There is no relationship with the woman who catches your eye. With your wife, you have a deep and long and meaningful relationship. There is no competition there. Yes, your mind may make the observation that this other woman is twenty years younger and has never had two kids. But that is all it is—an observation. And that observation is immediately offset by other factors, such as the fact that you love your wife!

In one small group interview, all the men agreed with that statement and added, in the words of one, "It is truly just an observation. There is nothing on earth that would be worth the price of going beyond that. I would *never* risk losing my wife."

In fact, if other women seem to want to catch your husband's eye, these men provided an ironic reassurance. One husband explained, "When a guy is married and his wife loves him, his self-confidence goes way up—and suddenly that makes him more attractive somehow. So if other women are *trying* to catch your man's eye, it actually means that you are building him up and that he adores you!"

SO WHAT'S A WOMAN TO DO?

For many of us, on these issues it would be so easy to move from understanding, to alarm, to the charge of the light brigade—to get anxious or suspicious of our men and get all fired up to change them. But in the book's introduction I said that these revelations are meant to change *us*. Yes, men can do things to keep their thought lives pure. Yes, men can do things to honor the women they love. But many books have been written on those issues by expert psychiatrists, marriage counselors, and ministry leaders. This book is for us women, alone.

So what do we do?

Pray for him—and for us

This is the most powerful and meaningful way to partner with the men in our lives, but it's often the most overlooked. There's a little verse in Psalm 127: "Unless the LORD protects a city, guarding it with sentries will do no good." We can work to help and protect our husband and our marriage, but in the end, that's the Lord's job.

Furthermore, ask God to protect *your* heart as well so that instead of feeling anger or hopelessness, you have the encouragement you need to "protect" your husband in prayer from the onslaughts of this culture.

Your husband needs your steadfast prayers more than anything else. And as we do business with the Lord, we will also better understand what He wants from *us*.

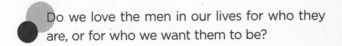

Do we love the men in our lives for who they are, or for who we want them to be?

Check your heart

As we consider any changes we need to make in our own lives, we must first take stock of the condition of our hearts and our willingness to support our men in the way *they* need to be supported.

Consider this plea, from the follow-up churchgoers survey:

> To accept the struggle I have with lust and encourage me rather than freak out and conclude the worst about me. The more I can reveal my weaknesses without being judged or accused, or without a major crisis in our relationship resulting from my transparency, the more I know I am loved for who I am, not for who she wants me to be.

And that should be at the heart of our response. Do we love the men in our lives for who they are, or for who we want them to be? Do we want to support our husbands, or to change them?

The way you answer those questions makes a world of difference. If you aren't sure you can address the issue with the right heart, you might want to spend some time praying and asking God for *His*, before you do anything.

Determine your involvement level

When someone is dealing with temptation, it is good to have a person to talk to and be accountable to. So once our hearts are in the right place, we need to consider how the man in our life wants to handle his vulnerabilities and whether we even want to be involved.

Just as some men want their wives to be a part of the accountability process and others don't, some women want to be involved and others really don't.

No matter what, marriage counselors tend to believe that although there needs to be an open husband-wife dialogue, the husband's *primary* accountability partner should be male. One male counselor told me, "It would be destructive if the wife becomes the police. Men don't need a critique but an encourager." I'm not sure any of us wants to hear a daily log of our husband's unavoidable temptations.

Become a support

If both you and your husband would like you to be involved to some degree, here are some first-step ideas. These are most appropriate for men who are *not* trapped in a serious struggle with dangerous or addictive behaviors (such cases obviously require more specialized resources, a few of which are listed at www.4-womenonly.com).

First, let your husband know that you are willing to talk about this and that you understand the difficulties he must face every day. Ask what you can do to help. Put yourself on his team to help him win this fight.

Daniel Weiss, from Focus on the Family, gave me great insight on this:

> The best thing women can do to help their husbands is to practice two of the most crucial elements of a marriage—openness and honesty. Things that drive anyone dealing with sexual sin are shame, guilt, and secrecy. If the guy has secrecy, if there isn't a safe place to talk about what is a real temptation for guys, then chances are it's going to get worse. The best thing women can do is to let men know that it is all right for them to share their temptation if they want to.

Next, notice and appreciate your husband's efforts to honor you. Keep your antenna up, and you'll be surprised by just how *many* daily choices he must make to keep his thought life pure in this culture.

Now that my radar is on, not only does my husband *not* resent my new awareness; he actually appreciates it. Because now I see the girl with the great figure—and I *notice* when Jeff is tense with the effort of "not looking." And instead of being upset that he was attracted, I love him for the effort he is making to honor me. Not only will this encourage him; it will encourage you.

It's critical to strike a fine line between affirmation and humiliation. No husband wants to be treated like your son ("What a good boy!"). But you *can* notice if your husband turns away from the latest Victoria's Secret commercial, give him a quick grin, and say "thank you." (And again, remember that every man is different, so don't jump to conclusions if yours doesn't turn his gaze away. Some are able to handle those commercials just fine.) Many women, when out with their men, will even say things like "What a beautiful girl," relieving the stress of his effort to "not look." (Of course, that only works if the attractive woman is like a painting, evoking admiration, not lust!) The key is to understand what is helpful in *your* marriage. Ask him what makes him feel appreciated or makes his struggle easier, and then do it.

A third way to be supportive is to recognize the common factors that make it harder for a man to stay pure in his thought life. Several organizations mention the HALT checklist: **H**ungry, **A**ngry, **L**onely, **T**ired. If a man is working long hours, is out of sorts with the world (or his spouse), feels unappreciated, feels like a failure as a provider, or is far from home on a business trip—if he is hungry, angry, lonely, or tired—any or all of those things could weaken his resolve. If you've ever found yourself eating the entire box of cookies when you feel unhappy, you can probably understand this dynamic.

Champion modesty in yourself and others

Let's face it, women who are totally clueless about this problem can also thoughtlessly contribute to it. After all, the images in a man's mental Rolodex come from *somewhere*—and it's not just from pictures. The eye magnets on the street are choosing to dress the way they do.

> Women who are totally clueless about this problem can also thoughtlessly contribute to it.

Unfortunately, because many women aren't visual, we may not understand what we are doing to the men around us—a fact that men find hard to believe, by the way. One father asked me why his cautious college-aged daughter dressed in a tight little top and skirt around a particular guy she found attractive. "Surely," this father said, "surely she knows what she's doing!"

"Yes," I agreed, "she knows she looks good. But she doesn't realize what is actually going on in that guy's head. What she's smugly thinking is, *He thinks I'm cute.*"

"Cute has nothing to do with it!" the shocked father replied. "He's picturing her *naked!*"

And *that* is what we often don't get. Many women are just longing for male love and attention, not realizing that the resulting attention is the wrong kind and has nothing to do with love. I guarantee you moms out there (and any dads who may be clandestinely reading this book) that your teenage daughter will *not* like the idea that wearing a tight little top encourages her male classmates to picture her naked.

Unfortunately, I can also guarantee that many adult women reading this book are unwitting fodder for the mental Rolodex of some devoted married man just because of how they dress. It's natural to enjoy being noticed, but he doesn't *want* you in there. You're cluttering up a good husband's mind and tempting him to dishonor his wife.

It is our responsibility to ensure that, as much as it depends on us, this doesn't happen.

PUT IT IN PERSPECTIVE

It used to be that a man had to seek out visual temptations. Today, they are impossible to avoid. So spend your energy helping him fight the temptations of the culture instead of fighting him.

Finally, realize that God doesn't make mistakes. One of my closest friends relates that when she was a new bride at twenty-three years old, she was very shaken up when she discovered that her sweet husband had this thought-life issue. She cried out to God, "Why did You create him like this?" And then she realized: God *did* create him like this, and He said His creation was *good*. We may be fallible, but we are created the way we are for a purpose.

God did create him like this. And He said His creation was good.

And God has something good in mind for you—and for the man you love.

Chapter 7

CHOCOLATE, FLOWERS, BAIT FISHING

Why the Reluctant Clod You Know Really *Does* Want Romance

Men enjoy and want romance but sometimes find different things romantic or are conflicted over their poor romantic skills.

Our culture often depicts men as a bunch of clods who have no desire to be romantic. The husband who buys his wife a belt sander for Valentine's Day is the hilarious backbone of many a television sitcom or movie. You may remember one amusing example from the movie *When Harry Met Sally*. Harry (played by Billy Crystal) explains to Sally (Meg Ryan) what goes through his head immediately after a sexual encounter:

Harry: "How long do I have to lie here and hold her? Is thirty seconds enough?"

Sally (shocked): "That's what you're thinking?"

Are men really clods when it comes to romance—or do they just think about it differently than we do? Do they really write it off as a big waste of time? Or is it just something they're happy to put up with as long as they get sex afterward?

> Are men really clods when it comes to romance—or do they just think about it differently than we do?

You might be in for a big surprise. According to my findings, most men feel that they *are* secret romantics who—like most of us—don't experience nearly as much intimacy in their primary love relationship as they'd like. Even more surprising, this desire is (in a way) quite apart from sexual intimacy. The great news is that our men long for connection, togetherness, and fun, intimate time…with us!

MEN WANT ROMANCE, TOO

I have to confess, I truly was shocked to discover this. On my very first test survey of ten men, when I asked if they desired romance *for themselves*, every single respondent chose "yes, very much"—and I realized that I had inadvertently bought into the popular notion that men really don't care.

As you can see from the survey, the vast majority of men actively enjoy and desire romance.

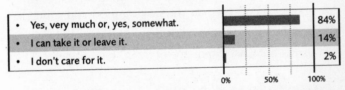

Regardless of whether you are able to plan romantic events, or whether your wife/significant other appreciates it, do you, yourself, desire romance? [Choose One Answer]

• Yes, very much or, yes, somewhat.	84%
• I can take it or leave it.	14%
• I don't care for it.	2%

As usual, these answers held regardless of whether the men were old or young, married or unmarried, and so on. As one representative survey-taker put it, "I wish my wife knew that I need romance, that I need touching and hugs as much as she does."

Listen to what one man told me about one of those romantically awkward moments we all recognize:

On our honeymoon, we were in the Caribbean and were at this dinner place with a dance floor, and no one was dancing. So of course, my wife says, "Let's go dance." I'm risking humiliation, but I go. And within ninety seconds, the dance floor was full. Someone had to risk it. Most of the women in the restaurant probably thought that the other couples didn't think about dancing until we gave them the idea. But I guarantee every guy in that place *was* thinking about it and didn't want to risk it until someone else did.

Men want romance, just as we do. In the pages ahead, we'll talk about how to get past the awkwardness and misunderstanding and move in that direction. And we'll listen to the *men* (every last Cary Grant one of them) tell us how to do it.

WHY MEN DON'T MAKE A MOVE

When I've told women that they're probably married to a closet romantic, I usually hear the puzzled refrain: "Well, if they want to do romantic things, why don't they?"

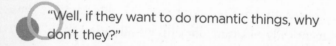

"Well, if they want to do romantic things, why don't they?"

The male responses fall into two catchall categories: internal hesitation and the "gender gap" in definitions of romance.

Their internal hesitation

Consider the enlightening survey results:

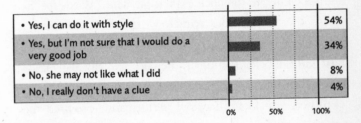

Suppose you had to plan an anniversary event for your wife/
significant other. Do you know how to put together a romantic
event that you know your partner would enjoy? [Choose One Answer]

• Yes, I can do it with style	54%
• Yes, but I'm not sure that I would do a very good job	34%
• No, she may not like what I did	8%
• No, I really don't have a clue	4%

Notice that a huge majority (88 percent) felt they could probably put together a romantic event. So in addition to caring more about romance than we might have thought, these men also had a better idea (than, say, your average clod) of what romance might look like. But the survey also shows the problem: Almost half (46 percent) feel unsure of themselves and aren't confident you'll like their romantic efforts.

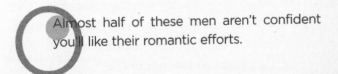

Almost half of these men aren't confident you'll like their romantic efforts.

As I spoke with the men, I tended to hear three distinct concerns that caused them to hesitate.

Internal Hesitation #1: "I won't do a very good job."

Apparently, many of us have overlooked the most basic stumbling block to his romantic initiative: self-doubt. Many men just feel clumsy in romance. As one guy said, "We do feel like clods sometimes. It's like trying to write with your left hand."

A single man brought up the impostor issue: "I try to just do it without being found out," he said. "No guy really knows how—they just play the game like what they've seen."

When you factor in how performance-oriented men are, this self-doubt can translate into hesitation—or doing nothing at all—even if inside the man is yearning for romance.

One man described the tension: "The flip side of the need for respect is horror at the idea of humiliation. I'd rather burn at the stake. That's why a man won't risk trying to be romantic. I'm risking humiliation if I do it wrong."

Another man explained his performance anxieties this way: "The reason men practice sports so much is so they don't get embarrassed on the field—so they don't feel inadequate. But there's no way to practice romance. So if they don't know how, they figure it's best not to even approach it and risk being seen as inadequate emotionally."

A man's willingness to take romantic risks may also be tied to how he's feeling about his job. A man who feels stressed and inadequate at work may feel particularly unable to risk feeling inadequate at home—in which case, it would be safer for him to do nothing.

Internal Hesitation #2: Haunted by romantic failures.

As you can now guess, if our men seem thoughtless or unromantic, they may simply be taking a safe course after what was (in their mind) a painful romantic failure in the past.

Because men often feel left-handed romantically, they are incredibly sensitive to criticism or teasing. One man said flatly, "You tease me about not quite getting the candlelight dinner right, that's it—it'll be five years before I try it again."

> "You tease me about not quite getting the candlelight dinner right, it'll be five years before I try it again."

Another man relayed this story. "I spent a ton of time finding this special present for her birthday, and I was really jazzed about it. When she opened it, she smiled and said 'Thanks, sweetheart,' kissed me on the cheek, and started talking about going out to dinner. I felt like after all that time and effort, I didn't quite get it right. Next time I think it will be better just to aim low and be safe."

Some men have the opposite problem—scoring a romantic success only to be paralyzed by the idea of having to top it. With my husband's blessing, here's an example. For years I was puzzled by a feast-or-famine trend where Jeff would sometimes go all-out to craft a romantic gift but would other times sheepishly give me a gift certificate. When we lived in Manhattan, he surprised me one Valentine's Day with a children's book about a little girl who longed for ice-skating lessons—just as I always had. On the page where the girl finally got her dream, he had taped a brochure for a month of private ice-skating lessons with Olympian Jo-Jo Starbuck at Rockefeller Center. I would also meet gold-medallists Katarina Witt and Scott Hamilton. I was thrilled and told everyone I knew!

But then I didn't get a "romantic" gift for the next three years. Not that I *minded*—I was just puzzled. Finally Jeff confessed. He was sure that he would never be able to top that Valentine's Day reaction, so he just shut down. "Guys are so competitive, and I'm even competitive with *myself*. I was sure that the next one wouldn't be as good, so there was no way to win." Thankfully, I was able to convince him that *anything* he put thought into made me feel special, which made it safe for him to try.

Internal Hesitation #3: It's difficult to change gears.

Even working women may not appreciate how tough it is for a man to switch from the fast-paced, highly practical attitude of work to the tenderness of romance. Many women see a microcosm of this every day when their man comes home from work and wants nothing more than to sit on the couch and surf through all 375 channels. My male interviewees have assured me that we shouldn't take this phenomenon personally—they just need space to relax and refresh for a while.

> The men assured me that we shouldn't take personally their need to decompress after work.

And everyone transitions differently. One high-energy friend, who travels with a stressful job, told me he used to arrive home and "bulldoze the house." Then he realized he wasn't leaving his work attitudes at the door and that "it was hurting my wife's feelings," he said. "Now she recognizes that I need help to transition, so she asks me questions, and I babble for about forty-five minutes. Before I know it, I am moving into 'home mode' because I have been able to unload my work issues in a safe environment. Plus I build greater rapport with my wife at the same time."

Almost every man I talked to said he needs to decompress *somehow* before he can think about being a romantic, loving husband. And if his wife can understand and give him that time, he'll be happier and more available the rest of the evening.

As one man wrote, "I wish I could make my wife understand that sometimes when I don't talk to her or act like a loving husband, it has nothing to do with how I feel about her. I just sometimes need to be left alone with my own thoughts."

Men are just different creatures—which accounts for the second main reason men believe we're feeling a lack of romance.

The gender gap in definitions of romance

One of my test surveys was of fifty men on a retreat. When I asked the question "Do you yourself desire romance?" one of the men answered, "Yes, very much," but added in the margin, "but we have different definitions." That led me to want to find out what definitions of romance women may have missed.

Redefinition #1: Playing together is very romantic.

Men want to go out and do things together and view that as incredibly romantic. Playing with their wives makes them feel close and loving and intimate; it offers an escape from the ordinary, a time to focus on each other—all things that women also want from romance.

Men want to go out and do things together and view that as incredibly romantic.

Here's a great insight from one married man:

Most married men don't want to abandon their wife to do guy things. They want to do "guy things" with their wife. They want her to be their playmate. It's no different from when they were dating. For a guy, a big part of the thrill was doing fun things together.

The woman who is having fun with her husband is incredibly attractive. If you see a woman out playing golf with her husband, I guarantee that all the other guys are jealous. Getting out and having fun together falls off in marriage because of various responsibilities, but men still want to *play* with their wives.

Once I heard this—over and over, I might add—I was able to see certain things in a new light. My husband is actually relatively interested in traditional candlelight-and-flowers-type romance—but perhaps more for my sake than his.

Talking to all these men opened my eyes to all the times I didn't fully realize that some activity Jeff suggested would have been romantic for him! In his mind, the activity wasn't just a fun day of hiking or a chance to relax and walk around a quaint little town nearby—it was his version of a candlelight dinner. Recognizing that made it much more fun to jump on the opportunity and appreciate all that it meant.

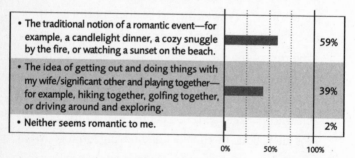

Men sometimes have different notions of what is romantic. If you take sex out of the equation, which of the following do you find more romantic **for yourself?** [Choose One Answer]

• The traditional notion of a romantic event—for example, a candlelight dinner, a cozy snuggle by the fire, or watching a sunset on the beach.	59%
• The idea of getting out and doing things with my wife/significant other and playing together—for example, hiking together, golfing together, or driving around and exploring.	39%
• Neither seems romantic to me.	2%

While almost 60 percent of the men on the follow-up survey desired the "traditional" definition of romance, a *large* minority—almost 40 percent—said they preferred the "active" model. Perhaps you, like me, have been missing opportunities to enjoy a romantic time with your mate just because you didn't realize it *was* romantic!

Redefinition #2: Romance without sex may not feel complete.

You can guess from the sex chapter that men consider sex a *part* of romance. It doesn't always have to be connected, and it doesn't have to happen at the same time—but trust me, it's in the back of his mind.

To make a giant generalization, women can often experience emotional closeness and feel that an evening is romantically complete without sex—while men often can't.

Consider these representative interview comments:

- "It is hard for men to delineate romance *without* sex. It's all part of it. If men are romantic, they want sex. If there were no moral or societal constraints, romance would *always* lead to sex."

- "I love setting up a romantic evening, but it is a lot of work for me. And I don't think my wife realizes that when I am being romantic, I've got a very specific endpoint in mind. So sometimes there's intense disappointment after all that work!"

- "The guy is thinking, *If romance is about feeling emotionally connected, and sex is my way of being emotionally connected, and we're already being romantic, then why not now? If we're going to have*

> *sex sometime in the next month, wouldn't now be a good time?"*

Another man brought up the unfortunate dynamic where a husband uses romance to get sex or a wife uses sex to get romance. But he provided an alternative view:

> If a wife only "gives" sex to get something she wants, that is so hurtful to a guy. Sex should not be made a payout after a guy works to earn his wife's favor. A guy wants romance not to somehow manipulate sex, but to reexperience the spark of dating, to reconnect after days of draining work at the office, to feel love and intimacy, to know he is wanted and enjoyed, and to utterly escape the crushing nonstop pressure of life. And sex can be a wonderful *part* of all that. Romance is all about escaping—escaping with the person you love and discovering to one's monumental delight that she too wants to escape—with me!

Clearly, just as we want our husbands to love us in the way we need to be loved, our men want the same. And sex is a huge part of making them feel loved.

THE POWER OF A WOMAN IN LOVE

Is it dawning on you just how much power *we* women have to change the whole romance picture? More than likely, we live with a motivated man who wants more romantic closeness, but who is holding back or frustrated. Which means *we* often hold the key to the quality of romance.

If you've been disappointed with your romantic relationship and have pushed and prodded to no effect, you've probably realized that nagging doesn't work. So how do we start?

Encourage him

Although a wife's appreciation is always needed, it is especially critical when the man is outside his comfort zone—which, when it comes to romance, is probably the case for half the male population.

One man was blunt: "Encourage me and affirm my efforts, and I'll run through a brick wall to please you. But don't just assume that I know you're pleased. I'm way outside my comfort zone. I'm willing to be a fool for you, but just tell me that I did good. And give me sex. That helps too."

Remember that many men view taking romantic initiative as a huge risk—a risk of "being humiliated" or "feeling inadequate." So prove to your man that it's *not* a risk!

When he makes an effort, it's *your* responsibility—and your joy—to demonstrate that it was worth it.

Even when a man *isn't* outside his comfort zone, he can become frustrated when we don't want to "go outside and play" when the opportunity arises. So next time he suggests something, don't tell him you really need to vacuum the house. Give him his version of a candlelight dinner, and enjoy your romantic time together!

Entice him

Just as men want to be encouraged, they want to be enticed. One married man relayed this interchange with a female friend who was wondering why romance sometimes dies off in marriage.

> Her: "Romance is the sense that you're still being pursued."
>
> Him: "But we caught you. Hand me the remote."

Many, many men have told me that whether in work or in romance, they are always looking for something to conquer— something to "catch." A key element in keeping romance alive is to keep giving our romance-loving husbands something to conquer.

Keep it fresh—give him something to pursue. Go hiking with him, play golf with him. Give him space when he needs it—and intimate attention when he needs that! Make yourself the kind of friend and lover he constantly wants to pursue.

Make yourself the kind of friend and lover he constantly wants to pursue.

Tell Harry what Sally needs

Several men suggested that since they can't read your mind, it is fine to drop hints about those romantic things you'd like to do as long as they truly are hints, not directives.

Take that classic Harry-and-Sally issue: cuddling. Because cuddling tends to be more important to us than to guys, a little patient reeducation may be in order. And this applies to anything you find particularly romantic that *he* doesn't get. "Help me understand why it's so important to you," one man suggested. "Help me see that as I romance you in *your* way, you'll be more motivated to romance me in *my* way."

This approach isn't a damaging, withholding-based model. It is learning to give what the other person needs and enjoying the resulting God-ordained fruits of that selflessness. One man's response to the cuddling example was, "Men can learn to enjoy a time of closeness after sex. And in this case, it is definitely in our best interest to understand why it matters so much to you!"

Keep him number one

If we let too many other priorities interfere with romance, it puts a damper on the man's enthusiasm. One of the most common concerns I heard is that we may unconsciously prioritize our kids over our husband. On the survey, several men expressed concern that "she spends too much time doting on the children" and not enough time doting on the relationship.

A man with three active children commented, "It's considered a Christian thing to do, to be with the kids all the time. But for me as a man, there is a sense of 'I've lost my wife.' It could sound selfish, but it's not. And it's not too healthy for the kids either."

One man said, "It's not just kids that steal a wife. It's the whole 'to do' list. Even helping others can get in the way."

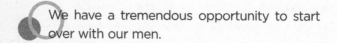

We have a tremendous opportunity to start over with our men.

That is the cry of a man who just wants to spend more quality, romantic time with his wife. What an irony, considering that most women pine for the same thing! We have a tremendous opportunity to start over with our men...and in the process rediscover the delight of the mutual pursuit.

Chapter 8

THE TRUTH ABOUT THE WAY YOU LOOK

Why What's on the Outside Matters to Him on the Inside

He doesn't need you to be a size 3, but he does need you to make the effort to take care of yourself for him——and he'll willingly help you.

WARNING! Before you read any further, pray first!

I'm not kidding. We're going to navigate some tricky waters here, and to get the most out of this, you'll need to be open to something you may not have heard before, while being protected from hurt. So take a moment now, and ask the Lord to shepherd your process of reading and absorbing this material.

● ● ●

Okay, ready? This chapter is about something our men

desperately want us to know, but feel absolutely unable to tell us...

> The effort you put into your appearance is extremely high on his priority list. Yet the chances that you know his true feelings are extremely low.

What I've learned about men's needs in this area has been life-changing.

What I've learned about men's needs in this area—including my husband's—has been life-changing. It has jarred me out of a dangerous complacency. Perhaps it will jar you out of yours.

OUT, BLIND SPOT

Call me naive, but I just didn't realize that the issue of appearance was such a big deal—such an *imperative* deal—for a guy. Important, yes. Imperative, no. Of course, having learned just *how* visual men are, I should have gotten a clue. But somehow I assumed that if I was out of shape, I was the only person who was negatively affected.

Then one day, after speaking to a mixed group about the other topics in this book, I was approached by a man I've known professionally for several years. I'll call him Ted. He asked if we could talk privately, and we found some chairs away from everyone else.

"There's something I need to mention to you," Ted said, looking uncomfortable. "I think women have a blind spot in an area that they really need to understand." Taking a deep breath, he spilled the beans.

"I don't think women know how important it is to take care of themselves and not to look like a slouch around their husbands."

"You mean, not to be overweight…?" I ventured.

"That's part of it, but that's not really *it*," Ted continued intently. "It doesn't mean you have to be a size 3. The bigger issue is that your husband sees that you are putting forth the effort to take care of yourself, for him. See, my wife is 115 pounds, but her weight isn't really the issue. It's not about being tiny. If she doesn't take care of herself, dresses sloppily around me all the time, never exercises, and has no energy to go out and do things together, I feel like she's choosing *not* to do something that she should know is important to me. And then it becomes a real issue because it affects her ability to do things and her self-worth and desire—and then it affects me."

That burden off his chest, Ted relaxed and chuckled. "You may not believe this, but it's not about whether we want our wives to prance around the house in a Little Bo

Peep outfit—although that would be great too. I mean, who are we kidding! But really, I just want to see that my wife cares enough about me to *make an effort*."

"THANK YOU, THANK YOU, *THANK YOU*!"

Ever since I decided to add a chapter about this issue, the male response has been astonishing. In fact, when I describe all the topics of the book to a guy, do you know which one he is most likely to seize on as something he wished his wife understood? You got it—*this one* (sex and respect were close seconds). Most of the men who hear about this subject thank me. "Thank you for addressing this, because I can't." "Thank you for saying what we are thinking but could never, ever say." "Thank you for taking on a subject that is so taboo, especially in Christian circles."

"I just want to see that my wife cares enough about me *to make an effort*."

A few things I'm *not* saying

Now, nearly all women have some form of body insecurity that we already worry about too much, and I'm *not* trying to add fuel to that fire! We're hammered relentlessly by media messages that we should all be perfectly shaped and eternally young. Thankfully, God didn't create us to be Barbie dolls. Those fake and impossible ideals only drive women into eating disorders and other unhealthy, miserable obsessions. This chapter is *only* dealing with weight, fitness, and appearance issues that we can healthfully do something about.

So first, let's celebrate our God-given individuality and body—sturdy thighs, small boobs, and all—and make the best of them. Men don't mind less-than-ideal proportions. In fact, many men I spoke with wished their partners *weren't* so oversensitive about their bodies.

> We need to accept how complicated and hypersensitive the appearance issue is for both partners.

Second, if you're one of those rare women who is a size 2 and convinced you're fat, be careful. You're probably delusional. This chapter is *not* trying to get you to lose weight. If what you read here puts you in a panic, please talk to a trusted friend or a medical adviser.

Third, we need to accept how complicated and hypersensitive the appearance issue is for both partners. Many men, for example, feel that they "shouldn't" care about appearance, but they do. Many women feel that true love should come with no strings attached, but still, we *want* to be attractive. And while we were delighted that he liked our looks during courtship, we can find ourselves feeling outright resentful that our appearance still matters so much to him now. (Do you see what I mean when I say *complicated*?)

Finally, please understand now, as I'll emphasize later, that this entire subject *isn't* about being tiny. It is about showing our man that we're willing to *make the effort* to address something that is very important to him.

So, with grace and good intentions firmly in hand, let's take a hard look at what men really think.

EVERY MAN CARES

Almost every man cares if his wife is out of shape and doesn't make a true effort to change. For some it's merely a wistful "Oh, for the good old days" sigh, while for others it's a relationship wrecker.

Here's what I asked on the survey:

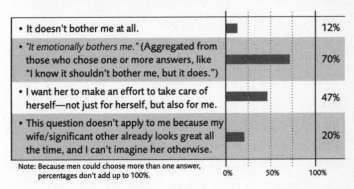

Imagine your wife/significant other is overweight, wears baggy sweats when you are home, and only does her hair and makeup to go out. She hates being overweight, but nothing much changes and lately you've seen her eating more sweets. What goes through your mind? [Choose All Correct Answers]

• It doesn't bother me at all.	12%
• "It emotionally bothers me." (Aggregated from those who chose one or more answers, like "I know it shouldn't bother me, but it does.")	70%
• I want her to make an effort to take care of herself—not just for herself, but also for me.	47%
• This question doesn't apply to me because my wife/significant other already looks great all the time, and I can't imagine her otherwise.	20%

Note: Because men could choose more than one answer, percentages don't add up to 100%.

Seven out of ten men indicated that they would be emotionally bothered if the woman in their lives let herself go *and didn't seem to want to make the effort to do something about it.* Only 12 percent said it didn't bother them—and even fewer happily married, younger, churchgoing men weren't bothered.

Once I understood this—and started making the effort myself—my husband felt safe to confirm that most guys do indeed struggle with this issue. With some trepidation, he gently reminded me of when, after our son was born, I used to eat a chocolate doughnut every morning. He said, "I know it's awful, but every morning when I saw those dough-nuts on the counter, my stomach would just sink. I'd think, *It's never going to change.* We guys keep our spirits up with the thought that some hope is out there—that things will change. So the chocolate doughnuts weren't the issue—it was that, in my mind, they said something about you making a choice *not* to get back in shape, for me."

Your effort matters most

Most of us can get paralyzed into inaction by the thought of having to look like the impossibly thin twenty-year-olds on TV. But over and over again, I heard each man say that what mattered most to him was not that his wife shrank down to her honeymoon bikini, but that she was willing to make the effort to take care of herself for him.

So I gathered my courage and asked the question directly.

Is this statement true or false? "I want my wife/significant other to look good and feel energetic. It is not as important that she look just like she did the day we met. It is more important that she make the effort to take care of herself for me now." [Choose One Answer]

True	83%
False	17%

0%   50%   100%

Look at the encouraging response: Five out of six men agreed—with regular churchgoers agreeing even more strongly. It's not that results don't matter—of course they do—but they will be a by-product of our efforts to take care of ourselves.

> What mattered most to him was *not* that his wife shrank down to her honeymoon bikini.

"For better or for worse"

Before we look further, those of us who don't believe in divorce may need to own up to a sneaking complacency.

Think how off-limits it is in a church setting to emphasize the importance of a woman's physical appeal. "God looks not on the outward appearance, but on the heart," we say, and expect our husbands to do the same. Because our husbands have pledged their faithfulness for better or for worse, and because we know "it's what's inside that counts," we can easily migrate to the idea that what's outside doesn't matter.

But what's on the outside *does* matter. And when we seem to be willfully ignoring that truth, our men—even godly men who are devoted to us—end up feeling disregarded, disrespected, and hurt. So let's try to understand why his feelings about your appearance can run so high, even if they're out of sight to you.

WHY DOES YOUR APPEARANCE MATTER?

One man reading a draft of this chapter looked at this subject heading and exclaimed, "What do you mean, 'Why does it matter?'!" Men *really* don't understand why a woman would have to ask the question.

One day I overheard my husband and my book agent, Calvin, talking in the other room. Jeff was telling Calvin about the time that "Ted" first brought this up—and the surprise I felt at what I heard:

> *Jeff:* "I was stunned when she said she'd had this great conversation with this guy and started sharing all the surprising things he'd said. I was thinking, *What about that* didn't *you get before?!*"
>
> *Calvin:* "They know it's important, but not how essential it is."

So why is it so essential? Here's what men said—when they felt safe enough to tell the truth:

"When you take care of yourself, I feel loved"

Since men are so visual, seeing us make the effort to look good makes them feel loved and cared for. It matters to them in the same way it matters to us when we notice our husbands making an effort to do things that make us feel loved—especially when they are things that are difficult or don't come naturally.

Consider one husband's honest comment: "My wife is trying to slim down right now, and it makes me feel like a million bucks. I know she's also doing it for herself, but the fact that she cares about how she looks is a total turn-on, if you want to know the truth. I tell her all the time how much I appreciate the work she's putting into this."

Because this area is so imperative to them, our efforts—or lack thereof—directly affect their perception of our care for them. If you have a hard time believing that your man really cares about your efforts as much as your results, here's a helpful romance-related parallel: If your husband truly puts effort and thought into a romantic event, do you really mind if it's not perfect? If it's your birthday and you come home from work to find that he has gotten friends to watch the kids, the house has been cleaned, and he has slaved over a meal, are you *really* going to care if the veal piccata is overdone? Of course not. You'll feel loved and cared for.

It's the same for him. If you make the effort to go walking three times a week, to do your makeup even if you're around only him, and to cut out sweet foods that you love in order to tackle your pregnancy pounds, he's not going to care if it takes you many months to reach your goal. He'll appreciate the effort you're making for him. *He'll* feel loved and cared for.

> He'll appreciate the effort you're making for him. *He'll* feel loved and cared for.

"When you *don't* take care of yourself, I feel unvalued and unhappy"

How does a man feel when the woman he is married to looks significantly different than the one he courted? After I tackled this subject in one of my newspaper columns, a twenty-seven-year-old man wrote to tell me he knew many men whose wives had gained a lot of weight since their wedding day:

> Shaunti, those women need to realize that their doubling in size is like a man going from being a corporate raider to a minimum-wage slacker—and assuming it has no effect on his spouse. A woman's

appearance is a simple yet important part of happiness in a marriage. A number of my friends love their spouses, but are not happy, mainly for that reason.

And being out of shape affects more than just appearance. Remember how much a man wants to go out and do things with his wife—and how close that makes him feel to you? I frequently heard how sad men feel when their wives don't have the energy or desire to do things together. One survey-taker wrote, "She is a very pretty woman, but she is not taking care of herself so she feels bad about her looks, she has little energy, and we are limiting our opportunities, such as going to a pool party, or the lake, or beach."

In a way, this issue for men is like the romance issue for us. Maybe it *shouldn't* matter whether our husbands ever put one jot of effort into romancing us. But it does. We love him regardless, but it doesn't salve the empty wistfulness we feel or the pain we may suffer wondering why on earth our man doesn't see that this is so important to us.

In a way, this issue for men is like the romance issue for us.

Guys feel the same way on this issue of our appearance—or at least our effort. It is critical that we acknowledge that this male desire is both real and legitimate.

"When you take care of yourself, your expectation that 'I only have eyes for you' feels fairer (and easier to accomplish)"

As we struggle with this hard truth, it might be helpful to remember that we're not alone: We're also asking our man to do something that is hard and goes against his natural instinct.

The man who originally opened my eyes to this issue explained it this way:

> We need to see that you care about keeping our attention on you—and off of other women. Sometimes it is so hard for us to look away. It takes a lot of work and a lot of effort. But it helps me so much if I see that my wife is willing to do her part and purposefully work toward staying in shape and looking good.

"I want (and need) to be proud of you"

Several men told me something like this: "I want to be proud of my wife. Every man has this innate competition with other men, and our wives are a part of that. Every man wants other men to think that he did well."

"I want to be proud of my wife."

Now, I'm going to share something that is difficult to hear. This two-part comment is from a close friend whose heart I trust completely. I'm including it because I've found it is truly how men think and because I believe it helps to make a critical distinction. My friend's candid comment:

Sometimes I'll meet a guy who looks just like an average guy. But then, if I meet his wife and she is huge and very out of shape and just sloppy, I feel so sorry for him. It sounds terrible, but my gut just churns for him. It's this "oh, I'm so sorry" sort of compassion. That sounds absolutely terrible to say out loud, but it is what every man is thinking.

But then sometimes I'll meet a man whose wife is overweight—but she takes care of herself. She puts some effort into her appearance. She dresses neatly, or does her makeup and hair. If she is comfortable in her own skin and is confident, you don't notice the extra pounds. I look at that husband and think, *He did well.*

"If she puts some effort into her appearance and is comfortable in her own skin, you don't notice the extra pounds. I look at that husband and think, *He did well.*"

I was so confused by this seeming contradiction that I asked Jeff to help me sort it out. Is it *looks* that matter, or *confidence*? "There's no getting around the fact that of course men are attracted to looks," he said. "But looks are just one part of the package, and it is the whole package that is important."

Since I was still struggling to understand, Jeff thought for a minute, then mentioned the names of two married women we both know. One is a very slender, willowy blonde with a perky personality. The other is middle-aged, no longer slender, with a gentle, confident air and a sharp mind. Jeff explained, "They look entirely different. But both are attractive—physically attractive even. I think both their husbands did very well."

WHERE DO I START?

If you're pretty sure this chapter was meant for you, but you want to run it by your husband first, my recommendation is simple and heartfelt:

Don't.

Most men are wincingly sensitive about this subject, mostly because they remember how wincingly sensitive *we've* been on it in the past. Think about it—if your husband approached you about this, no matter how gently, what would you do? Probably the same as I have done in similar circumstances: burst into tears. That is enough to make most men so distressed and uncomfortable that they will never bring it up again. One man who had dipped his toe in those waters before said, "I know that if I bring it up it will just hurt her feelings too much. So I'm going to preserve her feelings at the expense of my happiness, or satisfaction, or whatever you want to call it."

Your man is not likely to be completely truthful, even if you—in all earnestness—*want* the truth. Consider, instead, applying Jeff's rule (my own husband to the rescue again). It's a self-inventory that's been confirmed by pretty much every other guy I've spoken with. Jeff's rule is:

> If you are not *realistically* happy with your *overall* appearance and fitness level, assume he's not either.

Don't make him tell you that—both for your sake and the sake of your future together. (And for the sake of your sanity, note the words *realistically* and *overall*. We're not talking about someone who is fit and trim, but thinks she needs to lose five pounds, or is dissatisfied with a certain feature.)

A man gets very frustrated when the woman in his life endlessly anguishes about her appearance—but takes little or no meaningful action. Many of the comments on the survey echoed what one man wrote: "If she wants to look better, she needs to do something about it, not just complain about it all the time."

> Your man is not likely to be completely truthful, even if you—in all earnestness—want the truth.

At this point, some of you may be throwing your hands up in despair. Even if effort is really what matters, how, you wonder, are you supposed to add this effort to your many others?

Well, once you decide to take action, some very good news opens up to you. As it turns out, the person who cares so deeply about your appearance is, in almost every case, ready to be part of the solution.

Good news part 1: Your man *wants* to help you.

Almost every man I talked with said he would do *whatever* it takes to help his partner make this particular effort. And that was overwhelmingly confirmed by the follow-up survey.

Imagine your wife/significant other is overweight and really wants to make the effort to get in shape, for you. But her slate is already full; she has no time during the day, and in the evening she has to watch the kids or drive them to their activities. How much effort, financial expense, or additional responsibility would you be willing to take on so she can do what's necessary to get in shape? [Choose One Answer]

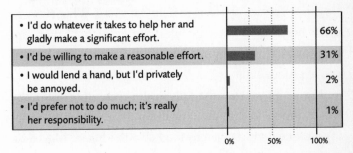

• I'd do whatever it takes to help her and gladly make a significant effort.	66%
• I'd be willing to make a reasonable effort.	31%
• I would lend a hand, but I'd privately be annoyed.	2%
• I'd prefer not to do much; it's really her responsibility.	1%

Only four men out of four hundred said they'd be unwilling to help, and it's highly unlikely that your man is one of those cads—er, unaccommodating husbands. Almost everyone else (97 percent) said they would help "willingly." One interviewee told me, "If a guy's wife suddenly verbalizes that she's determined to drop some weight and needs his help, any guy is going to jump to it! 'What can I do? Here's a credit card!'"

Almost every man said he would willingly help his partner make this effort.

My husband drew a youthful comparison. "Look," he said, "when we were teenagers, the guys were always busy playing football or whatever. But if our girlfriends needed a ride to the tanning salon, we'd drop everything and drive them in a heartbeat. We'd even give them money to go! It was in our best interest! And that feeling doesn't change as we get older—we're *willing* to help our wives. What changes is the busyness of our schedules. But even then, there are things almost any guy can and will do to help if he sees you're serious about it."

Maybe he watches the kids in the evening or drives the soccer carpool so you can go work out. Maybe he stops bringing a particularly dangerous food into the house. Maybe he cooks dinner so you don't have to prepare foods you're trying to avoid. Or maybe he agrees to go on the diet with you. (Jeff has sheepishly admitted that several diets he has tried were—at their core—veiled attempts to get me to join him!)

And remember, since it's your sincere concern and effort that matters most, you can expect to see relationship benefits coming your way very soon.

Good news part 2: There's a revolution in the resources to help you.

Over the years I've tried almost every diet under the sun— only to watch helplessly as the weight crept back (can you relate?). But now I've learned that almost everything I had known about healthful eating was wrong. No wonder nothing worked long-term! Thankfully, there has been a revolution in our scientific understanding of what eating well actually means (eating good carbs and good fats and avoiding bad ones)—and if you're like me, knowledge is the key to making a complete lifestyle change.

Without that knowledge, it is likely that we will keep sabotaging our efforts over the long term. Thankfully, several well-respected books are now available on what it really means to eat well and thus maintain a lifelong healthy weight. (On a personal note, I feel like I can stick with my new eating habits for the rest of my life because of the education I gained from *The South Beach Diet* by cardiologist Dr. Arthur Agatston.)

Good news part 3: God will help you.

You probably feel battered by all of this information, so let me encourage you: God will help you address this health and fitness issue in amazing ways, once you realize you need to.

Now that my eyes have been opened to the fact that my *efforts* are actually so important to my husband (and, conversely, that my lack of effort is so hurtful), you wouldn't believe the difference it has made in my motivation. I feel like the Lord has blessed my desire to serve my husband and our marriage by giving me a *permanent* internal motivation to have a healthy "temple." And I know He will do the same for you.

> God will help you address this health and fitness issue in amazing ways, once you realize you need to.

I hope you have read this chapter prayerfully, allowing God to give you peace rather than a knot in your stomach. God is a God of peace, after all. And He—like our husbands—loves us no matter what our imperfections are.

Chapter 9

WORDS FOR YOUR HEART

What Your Man *Most* Wishes You Knew About Him

*The one thing men
most wish they could tell us . . .*

We've come almost to the end of our journey together. But before I get to the final, most important revelation about the inner lives of men, I want to offer something from my heart as I walk this path with you.

Some of us may be challenged by what we have learned in these pages. These realities may not fit our idealistic or politically correct views of men. But just as we have discussed the difficult choices we expect our men to make, we must make our own. We can remain behind our safe, carefully constructed viewpoints about our men, or we can step out in courage to face the truth—and all that it means for what *we* must become.

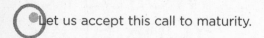

Let us accept this call to maturity.

Let us accept this call to maturity and receive this invitation for our generation to become the strong, gentle, godly women our men need. If we are willing to be molded by His hands, the Lord will shower us, our men, and our relationships with abundance. That is the way He works. He made us for each other. He is the Author of love.

And that brings me to the conclusion of our journey—the single most important thing you need to know about the inner lives of men. The response that surprised me the most from the survey.

THE NUMBER ONE SURVEY RESPONSE

As you now know well, I asked the survey respondents one open-ended question that they could answer however they wanted:

What is the one thing that you wish your wife/significant other knew, but you feel you can't explain to her or tell her?

Hundreds of responses rolled in, and far and away the top response was this:

How much I love her.

I was stunned. Here was a perfect opportunity for men to vent if they wanted to, or to share those things they wished their mate would work on. And yet by far, the largest number of those responding—almost twice as many as the next highest response—chose to use the space to say that they wished their wife knew "How much I really do love her" (or the cousin statement, that there was nothing he couldn't share because they had a great relationship).

When I told a male colleague how surprised I was about this, he said, "Men really do have an unspoken longing to be able to say or show 'I love you,' but they rarely feel successful at accomplishing it."

One man surveyed seemed to perfectly capture the way many men feel about the women in their lives, even if there *are* things in the relationship that need work. He answered that he wished his wife knew "how important some things are to me that I won't mention because she's more important to me than all those other things."

Men want to show us how much they love us and long for their women to understand what is going on inside, even though they sometimes can't explain it well. More than once I have seen men tear up as they read the draft of this book, moved by the thought that their wife might be able to—or want to—truly understand them.

So in the interest of understanding... the *Top Five*

In earlier pages, you saw the responses to each of the multiple-choice survey questions. But when the men wrote in what was *most* important to them, out of all the primary topics the top five responses looked like this. In reverse order:

- 10% — "I need her to understand my burden to provide/ how draining my job is."

- 10% — "I need more sex."

- 15% — "I need more respect, in private and public."

- 18% — "I wish she'd make more of an effort to take care of herself."

And number one....

- 32% — "I want her to know how much I love her"/ "There's nothing I can't tell her."

Out of the infinite number of topics a man *could* mention, to have so many men say that one same thing is astounding… and wonderful.

"HOW MUCH I LOVE HER"

I'll close by reprinting here a sample of the loving comments from the survey. We've talked a lot in this book about all those things your man may need, but intentionally haven't dealt with what you and I need. What we need, of course, is to feel his love. And if he's like most men, he really does long to show it to you.

"The one thing I most wish my wife knew…" (in alphabetical order):

- "After so many years, I hope my wife knows that she is the best hope in my life. We don't have everything that we desire material-wise, but there is so much more to life than that. I hope my wife knows that I love her and cherish our friendship, forever."
- "How happy she makes me even when I am stressed or down about something else."
- "How much I love and appreciate her."
- "How much I love her."

- "How much I really care."
- "How much I truly do care for and love her and the kids."
- "How much she means to me."
- "How great of a person I think she is."
- "I am very happy with my wife…. She may not be the perfect woman, but she is the perfect woman for me."
- "I have a perfect wife and marriage!"
- "I have a wonderful relationship with my wife and we communicate well. I wouldn't change a thing."
- "I love her and only her. It doesn't matter that our relationship isn't perfect—my love for her is so deep that nothing could break it."
- "I love my wife and want to be with her."
- "I love you. Please understand me. Make the leap to try."
- "I love you with all my heart."
- "I wish that she knew how much I look up to her for ALL she is—intelligent, beautiful, capable, sexy, creative, generous, and kind. It seems that not a day passes when she doesn't feel insecure in one of these categories (or sometimes more than one). I wish that she had the confidence in herself that I have in her."

- "I would like her to know every day that I love her with all my heart and would do anything it took to keep that love alive."

"I love her with all my heart and would do anything it took to keep that love alive."

- "That I am a sensitive man who loves deeply and wants to be loved deeply. And that I want to serve her if she would just let me."
- "That I love her more than she thinks I do."
- "That I will love her no matter what."
- "That she is the most important thing in life."
- "That she truly is the light of my life."
- "We have been together a long time and I hope she knows I will always love her."

THE HOPE OF ORDINARY MEN

In conclusion, one man provided great encouragement to every woman out there who wants to support her man in becoming all God intends him to be. "It is so true, that behind every great man is a great woman," he said. "There are a lot of men out there who are mediocre, simply because their wives will not support them and bring them to greatness. And there are a lot of mediocre men who are destined to become great men—who *are becoming* great men—because their wives love and support them.

"My wife expects great things from me," he continued, "even though I'm a pretty ordinary guy really. She looks at me like I'm a genius in my field. She respects me in public and affirms me in private. I love her. And like all men, I want to live up to her expectations."

May the comments you've read here and in the preceding chapters encourage you to go forward in your new understanding of your man, in hope, in confidence, and in peace.

If what you have read has been helpful, I hope you are eager to learn more. I usually have an extensive resource section, but because of space constraints I'm listing those resources at www.4-womenonly.com instead. The entire survey is also published at that site, as well as many other elements that were not included in this book (such as the follow-up survey and the hundreds of written responses to the survey question "What is the one most important thing you wish your wife knew?").

That said, I must list one "starting point" here: The "newcomers" section of Dr. Emerson Eggerich's website, loveandrespect.com, will walk you further down the important path of respecting your husband in the way he needs and will help your husband understand how to love you in the way you need.

CITATIONS AND ACKNOWLEDGMENTS

Citations

- Frank Maguire's story in chapter 4 taken from Francis Maguire, *You're The Greatest! How Validated Employees Can Impact Your Bottom Line* (Germantown, TN: Saltillo Press, 2001), 210–11.

- Jack Welch quote in chapter 4 excerpted from Jack Welch and John A. Byrne, *Jack: Straight from the Gut* (New York: Warner Books, 2001).

- "Not Tonight, Dear…" article in chapter 5 from Jill Eggleton Brett, "Not Tonight, Dear…" *Today's Christian Woman* 24, no. 2 (March/April 2002): 68.

- Movie, television, and music references:

  - Chapter 2: *The Natural*, 1984, Columbia/Tristar Studios, directed by Barry Levinson; cast, Robert Redford, Glenn Close.

  - Chapter 3: *Star Trek* reference from *Star Trek: The Next Generation* by Gene Roddenberry, episode #260, "Attached." The exact quotes were tracked down by Steve Krutzler, editor, www.TrekWeb.com.

  - Chapter 4: *The Lord of the Rings: The Return of the King*, 2003, New Line Studios, directed by Peter Jackson; cast, Elijah Wood, Sean Astin; based on the novel by J. R. R. Tolkien.

  - Chapter 7: *When Harry Met Sally*, 1989, MGM Studios, directed by Rob Reiner; cast, Billy Crystal, Meg Ryan.

  - The song one of my interviewees referenced in chapter 5 is "Behind Closed Doors" © 1973 by Charlie Rich, Sony Music.

Acknowledgments

This book required the help and input of hundreds of people, and although I cannot list them all here, they have my deepest thanks. A few, however, *must* be mentioned.

The first and second professional surveys that form the backbone of this book were guided and directed by Chuck Cowan of Analytic Focus (www.analyticfocus.com) and performed by Cindy Ford, Cari Peek, Kevin Sharp, and the rest of the team at Decision Analyst (www.decisionanalyst.com). My gratitude goes to them and to the team at Multnomah, especially Cathy Zerbe and Darrell Neet for the follow-up survey. (Thanks also to Reg Rhodes for his early help with the survey questions.)

I am so grateful for the honesty and vulnerability of the many men who were willing to be interviewed, and to protect their privacy I will not list them here. But I would like to thank Dr. Emerson Eggerichs of Love and Respect Ministries (www.loveandrespect.com), Daniel Weiss of Focus on the Family, Ken Ruettgers, and the other men listed by name in the book for their willingness to share their insight.

If this book is anointed by the Father in any way, it is because a dedicated team prayed for this book every day for nine months. I am so thankful for these faithful prayer warriors: Martha Abrams, Diana Baker, Scott and Tammy Beck, Allan Beeber, Elizabeth Beinhocker, Patti Benjamin, Steve Blum, Ann Browne, Brent and Polly Byrnes, Gerry Crete, Kimberly Crumm, Sean and Alison Darrell, Mike Deagle, Debbie DeGraff, Betty Dunkum, Calvin Edwards, Lynn Elam, MolliAnne Elliott, Jeff Feldhahn, Troy Ferrin, Nancy French, Natt Gantt, Katie Gates, Deb and Michael Goldstone, Corkie

Haan, Martha (Carter) Herndon, Judy Hitson, John Holcomb, Anne Hotchkiss, Victor Jih, Jane Joiner, Susan Kess, Kristen Lambert, Mary Laudermilk, Roy Leffew, the late Kathryn Lindstrom, Jan Maclaury, Sandra Maclively, Dan Maljanian, Denice Moughamian, Mike Owen, Linda Preston, Dick and Judy Reidinger, Lisa and Eric Rice, Susan Rodenberg, Roger Scarlett, Jim and Chris Sharp, Wendy and Albert Shashoua, Kathy Smith, D. J. Snell, Lon and Katherine Waitman, and Jewels Warren. My deep thanks also goes to the many readers on my prayer team whom I do not know personally, but who have also been faithful in prayer (and special thanks to Rachel Duarte for conducting a test poll).

Most important, God used a small team of people—mostly men— to actively shape this book. My eternal gratitude goes to these core advisers: my husband, Jeff (I'll get back to him in a minute), my book agent, Calvin Edwards, and the Multnomah team, including my editors, Dave and Heather Kopp, Bill Jensen, Don Jacobson, and Jennifer Gott. Also important were my parents, Dick and Judy Reidinger, my brother Rick, and my team of male and female "readers," including Lisa and Eric Rice, D. J. Snell, Nancy French, Dan Maljanian, Jim Sharp, Roger Scarlett, Ann Browne, Katie Gates, Sean and Alison Darrell, Julie Anne Fidler, Bruce and Sue Osterink, and others.

Finally, there is no way to adequately express my love and respect to my husband, Jeff. Dear one, your insight, prayer, encouragement, and steadfast support have shaped each and every book and article I've written, but no work bears your stamp as much as this one. You are an example of what a husband should be, which is why my greatest gratitude goes to the Author of Love, who gave us to each other.

THE LIGHTS
OF TENTH STREET

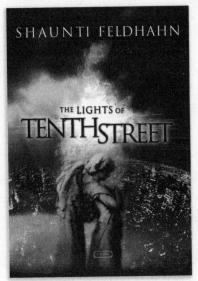

1-59052-080-7

The Lights of Tenth Street is a contemporary novel that looks at a young woman caught in the clutches of the sex industry and a Christian couple who move out of their comfort zone to come to her aid. It is written to give both faithful and struggling people strength to meet the challenges of our sexualized society. Men and women who feel trapped by sin, or whose marriages are struggling, will find hope and insight in these pages, as they are reminded that none of us are exempt from the seduction that is permeating our culture.

Dear readers—

I invite you to read the book that started it all!

The revelations in *For Women Only* actually arose as a result of research for my novel *The Lights of Tenth Street*, which followed a good Christian husband and father and his internal, secret thoughts, feelings, and struggles.

You've read *For Women Only*; now learn even more through the eyes of a male character. And enjoy what I hope is a compelling and eye-opening story about a young woman who becomes trapped in a difficult and dangerous life path—one that will intersect that of the Christian husband and his wife.

I want to share two e-mails I received about *The Lights of Tenth Street*. First from a woman:

I am a voracious reader. This is the best book I have ever read. Not only a real "page-turner," but what a message! ...There are no words to tell you how deeply and wonderfully this book changed my life, changed my opinion and feelings toward my husband. People have commented they see a big change in my life and it is due to reading your book.

And this one from a man:

Your book surprised me! Not even halfway through it I was closing the book and double-checking your picture on the back. Yes, I said to myself, it's a woman, but how on earth does she know that well how a guy's mind works? Your research must've been very thorough, but I'd say the real answer came to me as I checked out your website and read how you prayed each day and had a team praying too. Incredible! ...The story and the message were great.

The novel isn't just a further look into the inner lives of men, and it isn't just a spiritual thriller that I hope will keep you up late at night! It also has a strong message about the role of the church in the world today, and our responsibility to show the unconditional love of Jesus to the "least of these" among us.

I hope you enjoy the excerpt on the following pages, and that you go check out the novel that started it all!

Shaunti Feldhahn

Doug Turner tried to stretch out the tension in his neck and shoulders. He needed one of his wife's back rubs. He smiled ruefully to himself and reached for his coat. With the way this day had gone, he needed more than that.

He glanced at the bronze clock on his desk. Ten-thirty! Sherry was probably already asleep.

He headed for the elevator, his steps soft on the plush carpet. At ground level, he exited the elevator and headed for the door, his shoes clicking on polished marble. He stepped up to the security station and nodded to the guard as he handed over his employee ID.

A few moments later, Doug steered his car through the parking lot. He pulled up at the darkened security booth and waited while the camera sent his license plate number through the verification system. He tapped his fingers against the steering wheel. It was a lot quicker when the guards were on duty. After a minute, the gate slid sideways. Doug's wheels bumped over the pressurized grating that would sound an alarm if someone tried to slip into the compound as he drove away.

The dashboard clock read 10:45 as Doug pulled onto the freeway and headed north. His stomach growled, and a thought entered his head. He pushed it away.

A few minutes later, the thought came back. *Just for a few minutes.*

He gripped the steering wheel tighter. *No.* He clicked on the contemporary Christian station. A few minutes later, he turned onto another freeway and saw the inevitable signboard.

Just for a few minutes, to unwind. The food was pretty good.

Doug shook his head and tried to block out the signboard, but the small thought had become a vise grip, pulling him toward the exit. Just like so many things in the last few months. He didn't want to resist.

He took the exit, made a right turn, and pulled into the parking lot. He had a feeling of unreality as he stepped out of the car, paid his cover charge, and entered the building.

The music was pulsing, and the darkness enveloped him. His legs took him toward the light, toward the thumping beat, toward the flashing lights on the stages. He slid into an empty table and waited a moment as the anticipation grew, then slowly looked up at the nearest stage. His mouth went dry.

Ronnie saw the new customer sitting alone and sidled up to him. "Hey there, what can I get you tonight?"

He jumped and turned away from the nearest stage. "What did you say? I'm sorry...what?"

"Can I get you anything? You hungry or thirsty, or both?"

"Um..." The man straightened and smiled briefly. "Sorry, yes. Both. I'd like your buffalo wings, a club sandwich with your house sauce, and a small Caesar salad."

Ronnie glanced over with a smile. "Gee, for a man with no menu, you certainly know your way around this place. What can I get you to drink?"

"Ginger ale, please."

Ronnie looked up from her order pad. "Would you like a beer? Drink special? Our Challenger Tooters are only five dollars tonight."

The customer shook his head. "No thanks."

Ronnie smiled and moved toward her other customers. A few minutes later, on her way toward the kitchen, she glanced back. The new customer was slumped in his chair, not looking at the stage, rubbing his temples. His blue shirt looked expensive but bore all the wrinkles of a long day.

Ronnie found herself feeling sorry for him.

Doug sat with his head in his hands.

Lord, what's wrong with me? Why can't I break this thing? I've even memorized the menu! I have a beautiful wife and children, a great job, a great church—why do I keep doing this?

The music was pounding, pressing in on his brain, making it hard to concentrate. He sensed someone nearby and turned his head.

The girl up on stage was gyrating right at the edge of the runway, her gaze fastened directly on him. He was trembling. A moment later, a ten-dollar bill was in his hand, then in her garter. He took several shallow breaths as she gave him a big wink and turned to the next man along. By now there was a crowd of men around the end of the runway, all panting for the slender, circling figure. Doug watched, captivated, as she collected dozens of bills, then finished her dance with a flourish.

He crept back into his seat, and his hand brushed something on the table. His buffalo wings and ginger ale had arrived. He picked up a wing and bit into it, only to quickly lay it back down.

He groaned and pushed the food away; then he stood, threw two twenties on the table, and grabbed his coat off the other chair. He headed for the door, pushing past the bouncers, past a group of people waiting to enter, out into the cold air.

He jerked open his car door and tossed his coat on the passenger seat, then climbed in and slammed the door. He laid his head against the steering wheel and wept.

* * * * *

Sherry parked the van in Eric and Lisa's driveway. Doug's car was already there, parked right in front of her. She made no move to open the door but just sat there, listening as the engine cooled down.

Her mind had been racing through the horrible scenarios all day. He'd contracted incurable cancer. He'd been fired. He'd lost all their money gambling... He'd had an affair.

Sherry closed her eyes, praying a shapeless, desperate prayer. She walked toward the kitchen door and stopped five feet away, reluctant to knock.

Lisa opened the door with a smile and a big hug of welcome. Sherry couldn't smile back. She stared Lisa in the face.

"What's going on, Lisa?"

Lisa linked her arm through Sherry's. "The guys are in the den. We've got some time to talk in private."

Lisa's gentle grip was firm. She pulled Sherry through the kitchen, through the hallway, and into the small den, where a fire crackled.

Doug was sitting near Eric, deep in discussion. Both men broke off when Lisa and Sherry came in. Doug came to his wife, tense and nervous, and enfolded her in a hug.

Sherry tried to hug him back, tears of panic near the surface. Her voice was strangled against his shoulder.

"Doug—what—"

"Let's sit down, sweetheart." Doug gestured at the empty space on the sofa where he'd been sitting.

"I'm not so sure I want to." Sherry gave a nervous laugh. "I want to know what's going on first!"

"Sherry, it's okay," Eric said. "Doug has something he needs to tell you, and wanted us here for moral support."

Sherry looked at her husband. "Moral support? For—"

"Let me translate," Lisa said. "He wanted someone around to make sure you didn't kill him."

Sherry laughed and allowed Doug to guide her to the sofa.

"Okay, I'm sitting down. Would someone please tell me what's going on?"

Doug took one of her hands, but didn't look at her. "I...have to tell you something that I've kept secret for a while. Well, pretty much our entire marriage."

Eric cleared his throat, and Doug glanced his direction, and then sighed.

"Well, actually, our entire marriage and long before." He looked up, and Sherry was stunned by the fear in his eyes. "I have a problem with pornography, Sher. I've had it almost my entire life, probably since I was thirteen or so. It started off harmlessly enough, I guess, as a lot of guys do. But I haven't been able to stop it. It's gotten worse and worse."

"What do you mean, worse and worse?" She withdrew her hand from his. "You haven't...you haven't had an affair? Have you?" She put her hands to her face. "Please tell me you haven't—"

"No." Doug corralled her hands again and looked her straight in the eye. "No, I promise you, Sherry. I have never had an affair."

"Then what…I don't understand…"

"I guess I need to explain what…what it means."

Sherry listened, stunned, as Doug described how, in college, he would buy magazines and sneak them into his dorm room, where he lived with other Christian men. No one knew. He'd continued the practice after they were married, bringing the magazines and hiding them in his home and work offices, eventually escalating to hotel porn movies on business trips. He described how he had searched for sites on the Internet, seeking out films or pictures he'd heard about. How he'd gone from an occasional visitor to a compulsive one. How he would sneak downstairs when she and the kids were asleep, unable to sleep himself until he'd indulged.

Sherry pulled her hand away and wrapped her arms around herself, tucking her chin into her chest as if to protect herself from his words.

"And then I started going to strip clubs. I'd like to say it was all Jordan's fault for forcing me to go with him when we were on a business trip together, but that wouldn't be true. I kept it up on my own."

Sherry closed her eyes, trying—unsuccessfully—not to

picture her husband in one of those places, trying not to imagine her beloved, her best friend, reaching out to tip a gyrating girl with a perfect little body. She shivered. Was he thinking of those girls whenever they were in bed together? Was that the reason their love life had become so stale?

"Was this—" She cleared her throat and tried again. "Was this what you were doing all those nights you were 'at the office' so late?"

Doug was looking down, his voice tight. "Some of the time. Yes."

She finally looked at her husband straight on, and the tears welled in her eyes.

"Do you not love me anymore?"

"No!" Doug's gaze shot up, and he reached for her. She recoiled from his touch. "I mean yes...of course I love you! You're my *life!* Why do you think I'm telling you about this?"

"I thought maybe you'd been caught, and you had no choice."

He stared at her face, and tears appeared in his eyes. "Sherry, I'm sorry. I'm so sorry." He hung his head, and she could see the tears wetting his khakis. "I had to tell you because I couldn't stand not to. You deserve to know."

"How'd you get caught?" Sherry's voice was hard. "Where were you?"

"I don't know if I should—"

"Doug." Eric spoke for the first time, his voice gentle but pointed.

Doug clenched his jaw and closed his eyes. "I was at The Challenger, that strip club off the highway on the way home from work. Afterwards, I went to get coffee and ran into Eric."

"When? When were you at the strip club?"

"Last night."

Sherry felt as if reality had shifted, as if something had come and stolen everything she thought she knew about their marriage, their love for one another. She sat, silent and stiff, for a long minute, staring into the crackling fire. Then she spoke without looking at him.

"Why would you have to fantasize on those…pictures, those sluts? Why would you have to lie to me?"

His voice was broken. "I don't know why, Sher. I just can't seem to stop myself, and I hate myself every single time. I never wanted to hurt you! I've prayed; I've cried; I've asked God's forgiveness. And I've promised never, *ever* to do it again…but I always do. I'm hoping that by telling you, somehow, it will help me stop."

FOR WOMEN ONLY DISCUSSION GUIDE

a companion to the bestseller about the inner lives of men

This all-new discussion guide will help you explore the complex terrain beneath a man's confident exterior. Personal stories, fascinating case studies, and pointed questions will launch the conversations you need to open your eyes to what the man in your life—a boyfriend, brother, husband, or son—is really thinking and feeling. For women who really do want to understand, this group or one-on-one discussion guide is a must for applying all those "aha" revelations to your relationships with the men in your life.

Watch for **For Men Only** coming April 2006.
Coauthored by Shaunti and Jeff Feldhahn.

www.4-womenonly.com

If you want even more information about the inner lives of men, be sure to visit our website!

4-womenonly.com contains exclusive information not found anywhere else, including fascinating stuff we couldn't fit in the book. For example, you'll find:

- **The entire survey**, including questions not discussed in the book.

- The follow-up churchgoers' survey.

- The verbatim comments of hundreds of surveyed men when asked, **"What's the single most important thing you wish your wife knew?"**

- Recommended resources for women, men, and marriages.

You can also find **new and fresh content** on an ongoing basis, including:

- **Exclusive articles** by Shaunti and several key experts.

- **Online forums** for additional discussion, including online chat sessions with Shaunti and the men she interviewed.

- **"Ask Eric"**—a chance for women to ask questions and get answers from a representative Christian husband who is willing to share from his heart.

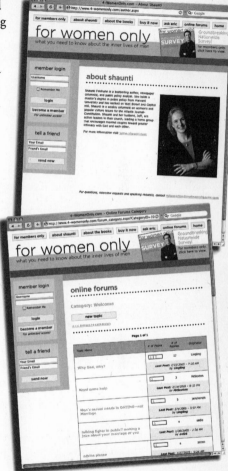

Join us today as we continue our peek into the inner lives of men.

www.4-womenonly.com

THE
VERITAS CONFLICT

1-57673-708-X

The Veritas Conflict is a riveting novel that exposes the spiritual battle at work today in our once-godly nation. Will Harvard freshman Claire Rivers sacrifice truth for an enticing counterfeit? Will she become a casualty of an invisible but very real war, or step into her godly heritage as a voice of truth and life to a secular culture? An intriguing read and a helpful tool for coping with worldly voices, *The Veritas Conflict* promises chills, suspense, and an inspiring role model for embracing our own assignments as God's emissaries in a postmodern world.

Dear reader,

Thank you for being willing to persevere through these fascinating and sometimes challenging subjects! I hope your eyes have been opened to truths you didn't before know, and that you have been encouraged in your relationship with the man in your life.

Many readers have asked how they can contact me for speaking, or to share their thoughts.

❖ For speaking invitations, contact Ambassador Speakers Bureau at www.ambassadoragency.com, write to info@ambassadoragency.com, or call 615/370-4700.

❖ There are opportunities for input and discussion with other readers on For Women Only forums at www.4-womenonly.com. (See the page in this book about the For Women Only website for more information.)

❖ If you want more information about me or my newspaper columns, see www.shaunti.com.

❖ Finally, you can reach me directly at shauntinet@aol.com.

While I may not be able to respond to every reader personally, I enjoy hearing from you, and I covet your prayers.

Grace and peace,

Shaunti Feldhahn

www.shaunti.com